THE WILL TO HEAL

A self-care guide to reflecting, resolving,
and embracing our past, present, and future,
with clear advice, faith, and expertise.

Emile Maxi

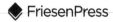 FriesenPress

One Printers Way
Altona, MB R0G 0B0
Canada

www.friesenpress.com

Copyright © 2022 by Emile Maxi
First Edition — 2022

ISBN
978-1-03-916131-3 (Hardcover)
978-1-03-916130-6 (Paperback)
978-1-03-916132-0 (eBook)

1. SELF-HELP, PERSONAL GROWTH

Distributed to the trade by The Ingram Book Company

$ 23.⁹⁹

CONTENTS

This book is dedicated to my wife, June Maxi,
the girl of my dream. We started our love
journey in our early twenties.
On July 31, 1994, we were married. Since that day,
after God, she has been my rock and my fortress.

ACKNOWLEDGMENTS

Thank you to:

My daughters: Juneile and Nicole, for your continued support and encouragement. You're always there to give me feedback when I need it.

My siblings: Suze (deceased), Rosana, Ascencio, and Mathurine. Mom died when I was only five years old. She left me in your care. Though you were all a few years older than I, you poured your life into mine so that I can be the person I am today. I am forever grateful to you for your care and love.

Mrs. Donna-Marie Francis-Bignall. You introduced me to Grief Recovery. This has been a blessing to me personally and to those who benefited from the Grief Recovery sessions. The knowledge and the experience I have acquired from the program led me to write this book so that, through the printed pages, I can help more people live a more fulfilled life free of unresolved grief.

ACKNOWLEDGMENTS

INTRODUCTION

FOR MOST OF US, life began with lots of great dreams and aspirations. But along the way, those hopes were shattered. Unfortunately, often the ones who shattered them are the ones closest to us, the ones we admire the most, the ones we care for the most. Why? Because when the heart loves, it pours out love unreservedly; therefore, when it gives so much and receives nothing or very little in return, it bleeds out tears of pain to relieve itself of the emotional hurts. It may even be scarred for life unless something is done about it.

When the heart is broken, the mind becomes confused. This state of mind-confusion results in the lack of mental clarity, an intellectual fogginess, and an inability to do what the mind was created to do—think positively and act rationally. The heart-and-mind symbiotic relationship is so complex that when one gets hurt, the other feels the pain.

When one is sick, the other is sick also. Therefore, you must heal your heart from emotional pain before you can heal the mind. Life's disappointments leave us broken, bewildered, and emotionally sick. They leave emotional scars printed on every fiber of our beings and affect us far beyond explanation. They impact our ability to trust, love, be assertive, explore, and live life to its fullest.

These heart-and-mind issues lead to constant emotional pain and unresolved grief, which then leads to anger, unforgiveness, resentment, verbal abuse, sexual abuse, physical abuse, emotional abuse, and social issues that affect the very foundation of life—our families, our society, and our world.

These unresolved griefs are at the very root of all evil thoughts, actions, and illnesses. They turn us into walking monsters. We act cruelly even to our own flesh and blood relatives and our lovers. They turn us into insensitive beings to strangers.

They take away our sense of joy and happiness. Since we can't give what we don't have, we become unable to contribute to the joy and happiness of others—if we can't be happy, we must make the lives of others miserable.

Our ability to trust, love, and care for one another vanishes, and our society becomes like a monster-ward. We walk around hurting each other with no sense of care or remorse, because hurting people hurt people.

Are you affected by all of this? Then ask yourself these questions:

- How can you restore that sense of peace you once had?
- How can you heal your broken heart?
- How can you forgive those who hurt you, for your own sake?
- How can you resolve your unresolved grief?
- How can your mind, which is a trillion times more powerful than a computer, go back to performing its God-given functions?

I've done my best to make this one of the best books about emotional health you can read, addressing the issues of both the heart and the mind. Whether or not I have succeeded remains to be seen, but I strongly believe that addressing these issues must be your personal top priority.

I have written through the lens of a certified Grief Recovery specialist and life coach to get you out of your emotional pain and help you start living a life full of meaning and purpose. I pray that you will find peace of mind through the pages of this book!

SECTION I:

DEALING WITH THE ISSUES
OF THE HEART

STEP 1:
EVALUATING THE ISSUES
OF THE HEART

*True happiness is an inside job. It is cultivated
on the soil of self-worth and flourishes in an
environment of mutual respect and affection.*
—Emile Maxi

Oct. 7
2023

THE *WILL*. NOTHING HAPPENS without it. Everything
starts with it. It's the only effective tool required to move
you out of any situation. God Himself requires it to move
you forward, and it's only effective and most powerful in the
hand of its owner. The *WILL* to be and the *WILL* to do! Have
you got it? The second is like unto it: *ATTITUDE!*

In his book *The Road Less Traveled*, Dr. M. Scott Peck
begins the first chapter with a heart-wrenching, passionate,

heartbreaking, real, and mind-blowing opening statement: "Life is difficult."[1]

Do you find life to be difficult? I do! Life was even difficult before the start of the COVID-19 pandemic, which hit the whole world in 2019. At the time of this writing, 2022, I believe that you'd agree with me if I said that life isn't just difficult but it's brutally difficult. COVID-19 makes it even worse. Only those who are very resilient will make it.

As a result of these difficulties, many emotional issues have arisen, so we can expect other health issues to surface. Why? Emotional health and physical health are linked together. One follows the other. To be healthy in the truest sense of the term, one must address the emotional issues to effectively deal with physical health issues, as often our physical problems stem from unresolved emotional issues. We can't ignore them, and failing to address them is psychologically, emotionally, and physically disastrous. What will be the result? A sick person—head to toes! The real question is: Which do we address first? It all depends on your situation. If there's an issue in your life, it could be work-related, a life struggle, or a stressful relationship. You take it to heart, and it starts to dominate your heart and mind to the point where you begin worrying.

Worrying over this issue will lead to stress, which in turn increases your blood pressure. This can lead to other physical and debilitating ailments that force your family doctor to prescribe medication to mitigate the harmful effects of the rise in your blood pressure, which was caused by stress.

This stress is directly linked to the emotional reaction to what happened in your life, and that reaction is now affecting your physical health and your ability *to be* your true self and your ability *to do* the things you like to do. Hence, it limits and restricts.

While your medical doctor may recommend medication, it's not uncommon for them to ask some pertinent questions regarding what is happening in your life. If they can link your elevated blood pressure to some external emotional triggers, they may recommend that you take some time off to reflect on and address this issue. Depending on the root cause, this might involve consulting with a psychologist or a counselor. If solved effectively, this will help to recalibrate your mind and heart, and hence your overall health. Knowing the root cause of the issue is of paramount importance in addressing your emotional or physical health. This leads us to ask the question:

WHAT IS EMOTIONAL HEALTH?

In "emotional health," we encounter two words: *emotion* and *health*.

- Emotion is defined as a "conscious mental reaction." This is indeed a reaction to something. It has a source. It could be something that happened within or without, externally or internally. It's a "state of feeling." Anger, fear, anxiety, happiness, joy, and love are all emotional words that characterize and describe the state of our emotions.

- Health is defined as "the general condition of the body." Good and bad health are words that characterize and describe the state or the condition of the body.
- The combination of the two words, emotional health, conveys the notion of being "sound in body, mind, and spirit."[2]

The absence of healthy emotions can seriously affect the condition of our physical health. Therefore, when we're angry, sad, anxious, or fearful, our mental state is impacted, which in turn negatively affects us physically. Likewise, the lack of physical health can also negatively affect our emotional health. When we are in pain, it's difficult for us to be happy.

When we are hurting, perhaps as a result of being disappointed by a loved one, we see ourselves unable to forgive, and it will affect our emotions. Our emotional health is under attack. This will shorten our lives more than anything else, as it has a domino effect. Who is affected by this symbiotic relationship? All of us! To negate this, you need to know how to take control of these emotions before they take control of you and create havoc in your body.

So emotional health plays an important part in our overall health. Generally, if you're emotionally healthy, you'll be able to control your thoughts, feelings, behaviors, and the challenges of life. It will be easier to get a good grip of the issues in your life and bounce back after a setback. You'll feel better about yourself and be better able to maintain good relationships. This, however, doesn't mean you'll always be happy, but you will be aware of your emotions and be able to control whether they are positive or negative. When overwhelmed, you'll know what to do to pull yourself out of that down state and/or seek help. No one is sheltered from this. It can affect anyone of us.

WHAT AFFECTS OUR EMOTIONAL HEALTH?

The negative effects:
- Disappointments
- Hate
- Lack of forgiveness
- Negative and unkind words
- Aggression
- Regrets
- Jealousy
- Covetousness
- Lack of respect
- Greed

The Positive Effects:
- Sense of fulfilment
- Love
- Forgiveness
- Words of affirmation
- Gratitude

- Contentment
- Respectful attitude
- Generosity
- Altruism

HOW CAN YOU TAKE CONTROL OF YOUR EMOTIONAL HEALTH?

The first five chapters of this book are about emotional health, or self-care, which means taking care of yourself. This is the most important thing you can do for yourself and your family. After all, if you don't do it, no one can or will do it for you.

What follows is a list of things that tremendously helped me as I sought to address my emotional issues. I call it my:

MY EMOTIONAL HEALTH CHART

- **Dealing with unresolved issues in my life.** This doesn't mean that I must talk to or confront everyone who does me wrong. If it's not best to talk to the person, I deal with it by way of doing a Self-Directed Grief Recovery Session.
- **Knowing what to overlook.** I've noticed that I have very little control over a lot of things that happen in life. This includes things that people do or say to me. For my own peace of mind, I must choose to overlook it to maintain my sense of emotional health and not allow it to bother me. After all, I can't control what others say or do, but I can control how I let it affect me.

- **Trying to always be aware of my emotions and reactions. Knowing** what makes me sad, frustrated, or angry helps me to be on guard and predispose myself to tackle it in a rational, calm, and positive manner. This also involves people with whom, no matter how hard I try, there seems to always be a personality clash.
- **Trying to always express my feelings in an appropriate manner. This entails** allowing persons who are close to me to know when something is bothering me. I don't want to internalize feelings of sadness, disappointment, or anger and add stress to my life. This can lead to health issues and affect meaningful relationships.
- **Trying to always think before I act.** I give myself time to think and be calm before I say or do something I might regret later. Knowing that I can never erase the words that come out of my mouth causes me to be mindful of what I say, how I say it, and when I say it. At times it's best not to say what I'm thinking for fear of causing emotional hurt in the process. This is where men differ from women. Women tend to want to know what a man is thinking, but the man doesn't see wisdom in saying it unless it ends up causing a problem. But it's important to evaluate your thoughts. Personally, I don't think I have to say everything that I'm thinking. Words have sharper blades than the sharpest of knives. Be careful of what you say. It can

cut and leave permanent emotional scars that can never be removed.

- **Trying to always manage stress in an effective manner.** I learn and practice relaxation methods, such as deep breathing, to cope with stress. I practice this several times a day, even before I fall asleep. If I'm in a stressful situation or environment, I practice deep breathing. It's so silent and subtle that no one notices. This helps me maintain a calm demeanor. I also like praying silently because I'm a person of faith.
- **Trying to always maintain balance.** I thrive for a healthy balance between work time, family time, personal hobbies, and rest. I make time for things I enjoy and focus on positive things in my life to maintain emotional health.
- **Trying to always take care of my physical health.** I exercise for thirty minutes, five times a week.
- **Trying to be mindful of my diet and get proper rest.** I try to eat a well-balanced meal and get enough sleep. I stay away from narcotic substances and alcohol so that my physical health doesn't negatively affect my emotional health.
- **Trying to always maintain a friendly attitude. I make it my point of duty to connect with family, friends, and new acquaintances, and I wear a smile to attract others to me.**

- **Creating my purpose and meaning in life.** I know what's important to me in life, and I focus on it. This means spending quality time with my family, caregiving, adding value to others, and inspiring people to do the things that inspire them. I spend time doing what feels meaningful to me.
- **Trying to always maintain a positive attitude. I like to** focus on the good things in life, and I forgive myself for the mistakes I've made in the past. I forgive others for their wrongs done to me. I ensure I spend time with healthy, positive people who inspire me so that I can remain inspired.

Evaluating the past is an important aspect in addressing our present so that we can live a fulfilled and happy life. Life is not static; it's dynamic. It changes every day. Hence, every day comes with its own challenges. I have taken necessary steps to ensure that I constantly prepare myself for the eventualities of life.

This evaluation helps us not just to assess the past but also to learn, unlearn, adopt, adapt, and address the different things life will throw at us. These will form what I call the issues of life. If these issues aren't addressed, they become unresolved issues. These unresolved issues shape our present and affect the quality of our life.

To help address the issues of your life, I challenge you to take the necessary steps to move one notch closer to a fulfilled life, one chapter a time. Don't be afraid to evaluate your past. It will help you to move forward, which is the purpose of this book. If you feel emotional and want to cry, don't suppress it. Let the tears roll! Quite often that's the way the heart best bleeds out the stored and unresolved emotions. Don't bury your head in the sand! Bravely deal with what you need to deal with. You are being healed. I even encourage you to say it aloud: "I am being healed."

At times life can be sweet, and at other times bitter. Do we have a choice in terms of which of the two we choose? If you're able to read this book, you're old enough to understand that the answer is a resounding "no!" However, I also want you to know that only one thing will make the difference, and that's your attitude. If you have the right attitude, when life is kind to you, you'll take advantage of it and make the best of it. When it's unkind, you'll rise above it and still make the best of what it offers. Everything rises or falls with attitude.

> The WILL. Nothing happens without it. Everything starts with it. It's the only effective tool required to move you out of any situation. God Himself requires it to move you forward, and it's only effective and most powerful in the hand of its owner. The WILL to be and the WILL to do! Have you got it? The second is like unto it: ATTITUDE!

As you read this book, chances are you're either coming out of a storm, you're in a storm, or you're heading into a storm. I'm alluding to the storm of life. It is real! It is brutal! It is merciless! Regardless of where you are in the storm of life, I'm asking you to read this book with an open mind.

Regardless of how hard life might be, you should not just survive—you must thrive. What will make the difference are the operative words I mentioned earlier:

- The *WILL* to be the best you were created to be and to do all that you enjoy doing.
- The right *ATTITUDE* to adopt. Without these two, nobody can help you.

As you open your mind to the content of this book, I'll keep reminding you that you're on a journey of emotional healing. I want you to say to yourself repeatedly: "I am being healed!"

> ...chances are you're either coming out of a storm, you're in a storm, or you're heading into a storm

As we read at the start of this chapter, "life is difficult." You and I can testify to this fact. You may ask how you can be emotionally healed in a world that is brutally difficult. I truly believe that you can be, and that's why I ask you to say it aloud: "I am being healed!"

Simply uttering these words doesn't mean that you're not stuck in the storms of life. You may be in a bad relationship and don't know how to come out. You may be experiencing ill health and don't know what to do about it or how to process it. You may have lost your job and are unable to put food on your table. You may want to try something you've always wanted to do but you keep hearing the voice of someone echoing in your ears that you're not good enough, or you'll never succeed, or you're good for nothing. Regardless of these thoughts, I want you to repeat again: "I am being healed." Being healed doesn't mean the absence of bad times or negative influences, but by developing the right attitude, you move yourself forward despite their presence in your life. To do this, you need to focus on three aspects of life:

- the past
- the present
- the future

It's as simple as that! However, while this may appear to be simple, it's not simplistic. The set of questions below will provide us with the platform to heal ourselves, regardless of how damaging our experiences have been.

- Where are you coming from?
- Where are you now?
- Where do you really want to be?
- How do you get there?
- Who can help you get to where you really want to be?

THE PAST MATTERS

Let's begin with your past. Sometimes the past can be so dreadful that we don't even want to think about it, let alone to put it on the operating table so that we can see all its ugliness. You may be tempted to avoid it, but don't make that mistake. You may be tempted to start with where you are now, but unless you evaluate your past, you may not know what you don't want in the present, so you might end up making the same mistakes and get stuck in your past.

Always bear in mind that your past is your greatest teacher. Don't neglect its lessons. In fact, we learn far more from our past mistakes than we do from our successes. It seems that life was meant to be that way. The great school of life gives us the experience before it teaches the lesson. We all want to be successful, but often we fail to accept the fact that failure is a part of success.

Failure and success are inseparable. One does not exist without the other. They're like the batteries that power your car; without the positive and the negative poles, there is no power. Since you can't avoid the negative elements in your life, you might as well make up your mind to deal with them and let them empower you. But you need not focus on its brutality only. Focus also on the lessons that can be learned. Arm yourself against its debilitating power in your life, and it will make you unstoppable.

> Always bear in mind that your past is your greatest teacher. Don't neglect its lessons. In fact, we learn far more from our past mistakes than we do from our successes.

USE YOUR PAST TO YOUR ADVANTAGE

When you look at your past square in the face, what do you see? This question isn't intended to harm you but rather to arm you. You may want to pause for a moment and write down your answers to this question. We're all in this together. Just like you, life has been brutal to many people, including myself, and at times we question the very reason of our existence.

The good news is that we can take the necessary measures to never allow the sharp edge of life to slice our throat; instead, we can use our time to provide motivation and encouragement to other fellow life-sojourners so that we can lift them up with the hope that they too will have the capacity and mental fortitude to lift those around them who need to be lifted from the pit of life. You cannot give up on life. So many people in your life's circle need you.

> When you look at your past square in the face, what do you see? This question isn't intended to harm you but rather to arm you.

At the end of this chapter, I'll ask you to take a pause to look at your past. If you do, you may see a lot of pain and regrets. Don't be afraid or discouraged by it. You are a brave soldier in this life battle, so let's march on to victory one step at a time. Remember, an army wins a battle because it conquered its enemy. The process of conquering is never easy. In fact, in the military context, it's life-threatening, but that's the only way to victory. In your context, it may not be life-threatening, but your life may depend on it if you want to live a life of purpose and meaning.

When you do take that pause, you may not like what you see. If not, let's deal with those items or elements.

As a certified Grief Recovery specialist as well as a certified life coach, my daily work involves helping people deal with the pain of their past and helping them live a meaning-ful life. Unfortunately, far too often I see people stuck in their past hurt, unable to move forward.

In their book, *The Grief Recovery Handbook,* John W. James and Russell Friedman, the founders of the Grief Recovery Institute, tell us that an incomplete past may doom the future. I hope you now understand why we need to deal with this aspect before we can move on to anything else.

In their Grief Recovery Handbook, John and Russell also advise that an "incomplete grief over a former spouse will dictate fearful choices. Incomplete grief will create hyper-vigilant self-protection from further emotional pain. Sadly, this excess of caution limits the ability to be open, trusting, and loving, dooming the next relationship to failure."[3] What I do daily in my line of work confirms this statement. What I bring to you, right to the palm of your hands and in the comfort of wherever you're reading this book, will hopefully help you just as it helped others take charge of their lives.

To help you move forward in life, even if you've been stuck in life's struggles, I will take you through some of the ele-ments of Grief Recovery and life coaching. You'll get a piece of both worlds as I attempt to address life's issues as best as I can. However, if unresolved emotional issues are affecting you, I suggest that you access the services of one of the many Grief Recovery specialists nearest to you. To facilitate your search, here is a link of their website:

https://www.griefrecoverymethod.com. Here you can search for a Grief Recovery specialist nearest to you. If you need the services of a life coach to help you turn your dreams into reality, I suggest that you do a Google search to find one near you. I promise that I will guide you through the pages of this book. Why? Because I want you to be healed.

AN INVENTORY OF THE PAST

As you evaluate your past, your list may include things like:

- Betrayal of people whom you expected to have your back.
- Having lost trust in people who let you down.
- Loss of trust in people in whom you had invested a great deal of love, admiration, and care.
- The person with whom you fell in love and married, contributed to their success, and who later dumped you for someone else, and now you're stuck in the pit of emotional and financial disaster.
- That person to whom you opened a door of opportunity, only to have been thrown out through the window of despair.
- The "Mr. or Mrs. Right" you met some years ago, only to realize that they suddenly became "Mr. or Mrs. Wrong."
- After always taking care of your body and eating right, you receive bad news from your physician that you've been hit with a life-threatening disease.

- That child you raised with great values who chooses a path contrary to yours.
- That job that almost turned you into a slave, only to hear the unappreciative words from the lips of your supervisor.
- That bright and exiting day you were experiencing at work only to receive the news that you were terminated.
- That pregnancy you carried for months only to give birth to a stillborn child.

These things are heart-breaking. As I mentioned earlier, life can be sweet at times but also bitter at other times. By now you understand that we have no control over life or what it throws at us. These things can either make us bitter or better. It's all our choice! What's your choice? Let's work together to allow them to make us better.

ARE YOU BITTER OR BETTER?

The list above may or may not cover all the things that might be going on in your life, but one thing I am sure of: we have no control over the past. We can't change it, but we can learn from it. This is the greatest lesson of all time, and failing to learn this has been the greatest catastrophe of humanity.

Acknowledging that we can't change our past mistakes shouldn't cause us to harbour bitterness, as that doesn't help at all. Bitterness only poisons your body and turns you into a bitter person, to the point where it destroys meaningful relationships. It can turn your loved ones and well-meaning persons away from you. After all, who wants to put up with a person who is constantly bitter?

No one enters a relationship because the other person is bitter. Therefore, your first step towards being healed is a choice. You must choose to free your heart from the hurts of the past, regardless of how painful they may have been.

One person we can learn from is Nelson Mandela, the former President of South Africa. In his book, *Long Walk to Freedom*, he tells us that "holding resentment or failing to forgive is like drinking poison and expecting the other person to die."[4] In fact, I would suggest that you don't even attempt to cast blame on anyone.

> Are you bitter or better? Bitterness only poisons your body and turns you into a bitter person, to the point where it destroys meaningful relationships.

The greatest mistake you can make is failing to learn from it. Wisdom comes through the gate of mistakes. There is no short cut to it. We all must pay this price.

In my line of work, I see people who are hurting. As the saying goes, "Hurting people hurt people." Sometimes they hurt their own loved ones without even knowing it. They're even unable to detect the signs of hurt—even when their children are hurting because of their actions.

I want to help stop the cycle of hurts. If you are hurting, before it gets to the point of hurting the ones who love you the most, I am here to help you. If you're not the one struggling, please give a copy of this book to someone you know who may need it. Far too many hurting people in the world today have no immediate plan to address their internal issues.

As we walk through emotional wellness, it's important that you identify the things that cause you to be bitter. Yes, you read it right! Identify them! Identify the area of bitterness according to your own list or the suggested ones below. Depending on how much you must unpack, it can take you a while to address each of the suggested categories.

- bitter with oneself
- bitter with a spouse
- bitter with a child
- bitter with a supervisor
- bitter with vocation or work
- bitter with a friend
- bitter with life

Don't be concerned about how long it takes you to complete this exercise. This isn't about speed. It's about emotional healing and wellness. You're doing this exercise only for you. You deserve to be free from emotional pain, so it's time you invest in yourself. Self-care is most important here. Unless you take care of yourself, you can't take care of anyone else. If you've flown in an airplane lately, you've heard the words: "You must put on your own oxygen mask before assisting others." Do not neglect your self-care.

Emptying your heart of bitterness is your first step towards emotional healing and wellness. It constitutes the very foundation of self-evaluation and evaluating the past. This is not to dwell on it but to learn from it so that you can be better.

When God created you, He created no space in your heart for bitterness. That's why it hurts so much when there is bitterness and resentment there, because it goes against your biochemistry. It's lethal and often at the root of most diseases. You need to get it out.

This exercise isn't intended to make you bitter but to get out the bitterness from inside of you. Talking or writing is therapeutic. It may be uncomfortable or even extremely emotional, but it's a part of healing. Allow yourself to go through this process so that you can heal yourself from your emotional pain. Cry if you must! Don't hold back!

> Emptying your heart of bitterness is your first step towards emotional healing and wellness.

There's a time to be thankful for the ability to shed tears. Crying is a good way for the heart to get rid of unresolved emotions, so don't suppress it. Let the tears flow. As you may have observed, after you cry, you usually feel better. Dr. Grace A. Kelly in her book *Grieve if You Must* admonishes us to grieve: "Healing is defined as total acceptance of, or coming to terms with hurt associated with losses, intentionally dealing with the pain and being able to let go and move on. Emotional healing is responding to present moments instead of recreating past hurts."[5]

In the *Grief Recovery Handbook,* James and Friedman state that "grief is the normal and natural reaction to loss."[6] But I also want you to know that while grief is normal, we can't continually be grieving. That's why addressing the emotional pain that brought on the grief is so important.

I don't want you to just feel better in the moment. I want you to feel better always by knowing how to address the unresolved issues of the heart. If we have the breath of life within us, life will always come with this mixture of bitter and sweet. We must not be delusional. We must always be prepared to deal with it. As an integral part of this process comes a very important question: How can we use life's bitterness to make us better?

We don't know why life was designed to be this way; I want to believe that one day we will know the answer. Until then, all I know is that the gold watch you may be wearing didn't emerge as gold but began well-wrapped in dirt. The gold had to go through a process of refining to be as beautiful as it appears on your watch. If you look at the crucibles you have gone, or are going through, you'll see that they weren't meant to break you but to make you. There is gold in you.

Don't allow yourself to be crushed by the disappointments of life, the divorce that has left you emotionally paralyzed, the person who betrayed you and left you in a total state of bewilderment, the death of a loved one that has left you empty, or the job that you lost that has left you broke. Emerge from the rubble of life's struggles, because you are that gold.

Don't underestimate the valuable lessons of your struggles, heartaches, and disappointments. If you adopt the right attitude, they will make you a better person. Because we all have our own struggles, they help you to connect with others even better, because it takes one who went through it to help one who is in it.

Some years ago, a friend told me about Grief Recovery as a resource that could be helpful to the kind of work I do as a pastor. But as part of the process of becoming a Grief Recovery specialist, I had to go through the process for myself before I could help others.

> If you look at the crucibles you have gone through, or are going through, you'll see that they weren't meant to break you but rather to make you. There is gold in you.

I knew I had a lot of unresolved grief and emotional pain, so I decided to go for grief recovery support first, for myself. I really needed help. I don't know about you, but I grew up hearing that strong men don't cry. I try not to cry because I want to appear strong, but let me tell you that during the session, which lasted for about one hour, I almost emptied a box of Kleenex. I cried till there were no tears left in my tear ducts. Over a period of time, though, I was a totally different person. I was a better person because I'd learned to use the tools necessary to deal with the deep and unresolved issues of life.

I now understand that while I can't change the past, I can learn from it and be free from emotional pain and unresolved grief. I have often said, "I now have an inner peace that I cannot explain. I cannot afford to lose it." This is all thanks to my Grief Recovery specialist. Once I saw the positive effects in my life, I decided to get the training necessary to be certified so that I could help others. There are millions of hurting people out there. How can they be helped?

I soon realized that I didn't have enough time to help as many people as I wanted to, so I decided to write this book to help more people in the shortest possible time. This book can go much faster and farther than I would, and at a fraction of the cost for a live one-on-one Grief Recovery session, either online or in person. Not to mention that you're getting far more than Grief Recovery sessions on-the-go. You're also getting life coach support on-the-go.

Usually, Grief Recovery covers a period of seven sessions, one hour per session for seven weeks. If it's done in a group setting, it's eight sessions for about two hours per session. At the end of each session, I always ask the people I'm working with how they feel now that they've gone through the Grief Recovery method. In this case, I'm asking you: How do you feel now as you're addressing the issues of your heart and the unresolved grief?

If you feel emotional pain from sharing the things you're bitter about, don't lose heart. It's part of the process of being healed. I am so proud of you. It's time you get rid of them once and for all. You have just earned a badge of honor for

completing the very first step. Not many people are as courageous as you are. Be proud of yourself.

HOW DO WE KNOW WHEN OUR EMOTIONAL SCARS ARE HEALED?

Very often, the scars of the past are deep and obvious.
Someone who was abused by their parents will have emotional scars. Someone who was abused by a spouse will have
emotional scars that may even affect future relationships. But
when they are addressed, even though there will be residue
of the emotional scars, things like talking about the abuses
won't be as painful anymore.

Let me use the example of a physical scar on the surface
of your skin. After properly taking care of a cut, it will heal.
Once it's properly healed, touching it won't trigger any sensa-
tion of physical pain, even months or years later. Then you'll
know that it has been properly healed. If, however, you were
to touch it and you flinch, you'd know it has not yet been
healed. Similarly, if your emotional issues still negatively
affect you whenever you talk about them or when they flash
through your mind, you've likely not yet been healed emotionally. Then you need to seek help by using the services of
a Grief Recovery specialist, because you're still grieving. The
issue is still unresolved in your mind and heart.

Don't just leave it to time. Sometimes you hear the phrase,
"Time heals all wounds." It's not true. Time heals nothing. It's
what you do within the time that heals. Don't forget this! You
may never have to speak to the person who inflicted the hurt,

but you need to settle it in your heart. Chances are that if you were to speak to the person about it, you'd get hurt again and again. Don't make that mistake. You need to settle it in your heart for your own good and emotional freedom. <u>Don't even dwell on the emotional pain.</u> The more you dwell on it, the more reasons you'll have to dwell on it. You're only perpetuating the pain and pushing yourself further and further into emotional disaster. Once you've dealt with the past, there's no need to rehash it. Leave it behind! Bury it once and for all.

Your present life may not be what you anticipated it to be because of all the things you've gone through. It may even affect how you view the future. Don't despair! There is hope! Let's move into the present and assess it. It may take you a while to fully get over the hurts of the past, but you must always remind yourself that you need to do it for your own sake. The only person who is suffering is you. Therefore, you must make that choice to let go. You deserve to be free. Let's take the next step towards emotional health and wellness by assessing your present state of mind and happiness.

> The only person who is suffering is you. Therefore, you must make that choice to let go. You deserve to be free.

CHAPTER SUMMARY AND ACTION STEP

In this chapter, we evaluated the past by looking at it square in the face. But we don't want to remain in the past. We need to move forward, which will require the *will* to do so and also the right ***attitude***.

You need to ask yourself two questions as you embark on this emotional health and wellness journey:

- Do I possess the **WILL** required to move forward?
- Do I possess the right **ATTITUDE** required to be able to soar to higher heights?

The *will* gives us the motivation to get unstuck, and it keeps us going. But it requires the right attitude to take us to an altitude. Your attitude will determine your altitude. Your past, regardless of how ugly it may have been in your scale of self-evaluation, should not discourage you but rather motivate you to press on. You must make a conscious decision to get out from the pain of the past. You are where you are today because of your *will* and determination or the lack thereof. You can go higher. You must determine within yourself that you can go higher. You must go higher! You will go higher! Nothing will stop you!

Are you committed to holding on to the *will* to thrive and develop the right *attitude* to reach your aspired altitude?

NOW IT'S YOUR TURN TO DO YOUR EMOTIONAL HEALTH CHART

Earlier, I shared my emotional chart with you—the things I do to maintain my emotional health. It's now your turn to make your list. It's all about self-care, so I want to be sure that you're not just reading my book but that I'm helping you to be emotionally healthy and happy.

If you're not where you'd like to be, don't worry. There was a time when I was way down in the ditch, but by reading lots of books on the subject and working on myself, I managed to pull myself up to the level of peace, contentment, and happiness. And so can you! Go ahead, write down yours!

To facilitate your progress, I have created the sheet below with two columns. One is to describe where you are now, and the other to describe where you want to be. You can modify it or create your own. Whatever works best for you, go for it! The two columns would look like this:

EMOTIONAL HEALTH CHART GUIDE
- To help you assess your own emotional health, you may want to refer to the section that deals with the things that affect our emotions. *p - 11*
- To help you create your own desired emotional health, you may want to refer to the section titled "My Emotional Health Chart." *p - 12*
- On the next page in column 1, list your Current Emotional Health and then your Desired Emotional Health in column 2.

EMOTIONAL HEALTH CHART

COLUMN 1	COLUMN 2
CURRENT EMOTIONAL HEALTH	DESIRED EMOTIONAL HEALTH

STEP 2:
ASSESSING THE PRESENT

*It's not what happened to you that matters the
most but rather what happens within you.*
—Emile Maxi

BILL KEANE, SAID: "YESTERDAY is history, tomorrow
is a mystery, today is a gift of God, which is why we call it
the present."[1]

Mother Theresa said: "Yesterday is gone. Tomorrow is yet
to come. We have today only. Let us begin."[2]

Mahatma Gandhi said: "The future depends on what you
do today."[3]

Albert Camus said: "Real generosity towards the future
lies in giving all to the present."[4]

I'd like to begin this chapter by making this statement: it's
not what happened to you that matters the most but rather

what happens within you. Hence, you need to release your-self of the damaging effects of the past so that you can use the present as a launching pad to a very bright future.

Let us now address the issues of the present. We all hope for a brighter future, but it can only be bright if it's created. The future depends on today's choices. What we experience today is largely a direct result of past choices; therefore, don't neglect the things you're engaged in now, because you will reap its fruits in the future—whether good or bad, positive or negative.

We're making progress, are we not? We're now going to lay the foundation for a great future. Yes, you read it right. Your future is going to be great. That's why we need to spend time assessing the present; after all, the present is all we have. Eckhart Tolle in his book *The Power of Now: A Guide to Spiritual Enlightenment* says this: "Accept—then act. Whatever the present moment contains, accept it as if you had chosen it. Always work with it, not against it. Make it your friend and ally, not your enemy. This will miraculously transform your whole life." He further says: "Die to the past every moment. You don't need it. Only refer to it when it is absolutely relevant to the present. Feel the power of this moment and the fullness of being. Feel your presence."[5] Don't put your past emotional luggage on the scale of the present. The result will be skewed.

> Do not put your past emotional luggage on the scale of the present. The result will be skewed.

You may not be feeling your best at the present, considering your past, your past doesn't have to define who you really are at the present. It's true that the way we behave today has its roots in the way we were treated in the past and what happened to us. Your past may be filled with verbal, physical, and emotional abuse, so your self-esteem is at its lowest. But it doesn't have to remain that way.

Though an adult now, maybe you're still hearing the voice of someone who was part of your formative years, echoing in your ears some emotionally damaging words. You may be out of an abusive relationship, but the past abuse is still present in your life and affecting your level of assertiveness, or even your ability to thrive in a relationship or life in general. You may have been fired from your job and unable to get another job that gives you that sense of joy and fulfillment. All these things may contribute to making you feel stuck.

> You may not be feeling your best at the present, considering your past. Remember, your past does not have to define who you really are.

Do not despair; this is the sole purpose of this book. I'd like to ask you to repeat the same words we started with in Chapter One: "I am being healed." I want you to say it and believe it. I've known a lot of successful people who believed in themselves and in their ability to achieve great things, even though others didn't. But because they believed in themselves, they were able to go against the odds and became successful.

However, I have never seen a successful person who didn't believe in himself or herself. Therefore, to heal yourself from emotional pain and abuse, you must believe in yourself and your ability to make it happen. It must come from within. Hence, the use of the same words we've been talking about: the *will* to be and the *will* to do. The second is like unto it: *the right attitude*. You must believe in your abilities to pull yourself out from under the rubble of life's struggles, and I'm here to encourage you. But my encouragement can only make it happen if you can find these words from within you: the *will* and the right *attitude*.

You may be stuck, but you're unrelenting. You may be shattered, but you're not broken. None of these things can stop you from reaching your full potential if you possess the will and the right attitude. The only person who can stop you is you. Please don't put this book down. Stay with me. I'm here to inspire you to become what you have always dreamt of for your life.

THE PRESENT—WHAT DOES IT LOOK LIKE TO YOU?

In this chapter, we'll look at and deal with the areas of your life with unresolved issues so that we can address them as we continue with the process of emotional healing.

> You may be stuck, but you're unrelenting. You may be shattered, but you're not broken.

38

So far, we've dealt with the past, mainly the past hurts that hold us hostage. You can't enjoy life because of them, and your self-confidence is down in the mud because of them. They will stay and ruin your potential for a fulfilled life if you don't free yourself from unresolved issues. And you'll be glad you did! Go and find that *will*—that's your first tool. Go and find that right *attitude*—that's your second tool. They are right there inside of you and at your disposal. Once you have them, everything else will follow.

Many people can't move forward because they prefer to suppress their hurts. Always bear this in mind when it comes to our emotions; whatever is buried alive stays alive and scares the life out of us like a walking zombie. That's what keeps haunting us and affects even our relationships and our happiness.

> You may be stuck, but you're unrelenting. None of these things can stop you from reaching your full potential if you possess the will and the right attitude. The only person who can stop you is you.

Our lives are shaped by three components: the past, the present, and the future. It's an undeniable triangle. The present reality is shaped by past decisions, and the future is made in the laboratory of the present. The good news is that although the present reflects past decisions, our future doesn't always have to be determined by it, if we can address it. We can start afresh right now. We can turn the misfortunes of the past into fortunes of the present, even though we often had nothing to do with the misfortunes of the past. They may have been hereditary, genetic, or societal. If for any reason you did contribute to your own misfortunes and are now paying the consequences, at least you can learn from them. You now know what you don't want and what not to do because the price of your mistakes is too painful. Mistake is the price we pay for obtaining wisdom.

> The present reality is shaped by past decisions, and the future is made in the laboratory of the present.

One thing of vital importance when assessing and addressing your present state is forgiveness. Take a moment to reflect on the following:

- How happy or unhappy are you with your present life?
- If you're unhappy, what is the cause of your unhappiness?
- Is your present state of mind and unhappiness due to the fact that you are holding grudges?
- Have you forgiven yourself for your past mistakes and decisions?
- Have you forgiven others for hurting you?
- Do you feel stuck as the result of unresolved emotional issues?

If your answers are in the negative, you need to address them to be able to heal yourself and move forward. I'll walk you through it, and I strongly encourage you to forgive yourself and anyone else who may have caused you misfortune.

Forgiveness is a gift you give to yourself. It's all about you, not the person who hurts you.

> We can turn the misfortunes of the past
> into fortunes of the present.

In chapter one, we dealt with assessing the past. Now we need to assess the present so that we can pass into action. The action word here is "forgiveness." I slowly introduced this concept because sometimes we don't want to forgive, as unforgiveness seems to be the only weapon we have left that we think we can "use" to punish the perpetuator of the wrong. I've heard this far too often in Grief Recovery sessions. If you're of that opinion, let me disarm you right now of that powerful weapon. Unforgiveness, or refusal to forgive, will destroy you much faster than you can fathom. If unforgiveness isn't destroyed, it will produce something with the potential to destroy you faster than any cancer, and it may be the root cause of many physical ailments: *anger*.

ASSESSING THE PRESENT

> Mistake is the price we pay for obtaining wisdom.

Just as I do in Grief Recovery sessions, I'm going to do with you—give you an opportunity to let go of this anger and, by extension, forgive. In chapter one, I asked you to list the bitterness. Here I want you to do something with anger, the fruit of bitterness: exercise forgiveness.

Your emotional health is directly linked to your ability to forgive because forgiveness produces emotional freedom, which produces healing. This can mean emotional, psychological, as well as physical healing. Therefore, unforgiveness produces the opposite – sickness. This can mean emotional, psychological, as well as physical sickness.

Can you be healed by granting forgiveness? Yes, you can! You can be healed from the emotional pain and possibly the physical pain brought on by the hurts and unresolved grief.

Can you be healed by confessing your own faults? Yes, you can! What does confession have to do with healing? Confession is recognizing that we did something wrong to somebody and are sorry about it, so we decide to ask for forgiveness.

The act of asking for forgiveness is more powerful than any prescription drug you may be taking for ailments brought on by the lack of granting it. Therefore, when you grant forgiveness, even when it's not asked for, you, the victim, stand to reap the emotional benefits. You will feel emotionally emancipated!

How can this be done? It's going to be done by way of writing a letter. According to the *Grief Recovery Handbook*, this letter is called a Completion Letter. It's intended to bring completion to the pain brought on you by your past hurts and unresolved grief—the things that were said or were never said, and the things that were done or were never done.

> The act of asking for and granting forgiveness is more powerful than any prescription drug you may be taking for ailments brought on by the lack of granting it.

TEMPORARY COPING SKILLS

What happens when we continually live in a state of unforgiveness and unresolved grief? We cannot reach our full potential. We survive, but we don't thrive. We limit ourselves from being who God created us to be, and we develop coping skills to get by. These coping skills are only short-term mechanisms to help us pacify the hurts and our true emotions, and they don't give us a long-lasting solution.

James and Friedman call these STERBS-"Short-Term Energy Relieving Behaviors."[6] Therefore, our STERBS can be but are not limited to:

- Food
- Alcohol and Drugs
- Anger
- Exercise
- Fantasy (movies, TV, books)
- Isolation
- Sex
- Shopping (humorously called retail therapy)
- Workaholism

These unresolved issues produce grief, which is emotional. At times, the hurt is so deep you can hardly describe it, yet you can cut through it with a knife. You can feel and experience its emotional consequences. It is brutally painful. The unresolved grief might be causing the emotional havoc in your life, so you need to address it! It's very important that you identify the Short-Term Energy Relieving Behaviors in your life.

Very often, these STERBS create more problems. You need to replace them with proper and long-lasting coping mechanisms. In short, you need to resolve the unresolved issues.

To help you understand grief, I'd like to bring two key definitions to your attention.

DEFINITIONS OF GRIEF

The Grief Recovery Handbook defines grief in two ways: "Grief is the normal and natural reaction to loss of any kind."[7] Sometimes we're led to believe that we only grieve as the result of the death of a loved one. That's absolutely not true. One may grieve because of loss of trust, health, a romantic relationship, or a pet. They might also grieve over a divorce, separation, and of course a death. You can grieve over anything that breaks your heart.

The second definition described in the Grief Recovery Handbook is that "grief is the conflicting feeling caused by the end of or change in a familiar pattern of behaviour."

> Therefore, when you grant forgiveness, even when it is not asked for, you, the victim, stand to reap the emotional benefits. You will feel emotionally free and emancipated!

This one demands some clarification, right? Let's say you're in an abusive relationship that's damaging to you emotionally or even physically. You know you need to get out of that relationship because it's toxic and is destroying you. You finally get out, and while out you're happy that finally you're free of it. But at the same time you miss your partner. Do you see the conflicting feeling?

Unfortunately, that state of sadness brings a lot of people back into the same abusive relationship, or they jump into another one. It also has the potential to make that person afraid of being hurt again, so they may never want to try another relationship. Dealing with unresolved grief may help you address your own fears and prepare you for a brighter future.

Let's say you have a loved-one who is sick and suffering a lot. Finally, the person dies. You're sad and are experiencing a lot of emotional distress. On one hand, you're happy because the person isn't suffering anymore, but on the other, you're sad and still miss the person. Do you see the conflicting feelings?

If, however, in either of these scenarios you have a lot of stored emotions that you didn't get to express as part of your healing process, you could end up with lots of stored emotions, or unresolved issues. We all have unsolved issues, and if they remain unsolved, they can destroy our state of joy and happiness, which in turn affects us emotionally and impairs our ability to fully enjoy a meaningful relationship, perform well at work, and even be effective and successful in what we do.

This is why I want to take you through this process, addressing the issues of the heart—the unresolved issues in your life—before I can assist you in addressing the issues of the mind and effectively move you forward towards your goals.

Very often, failing to address the issues of the heart leads to substance abuse, addiction, suicidal thoughts, constant anger, a deep sense of unhappiness, and unfulfilled and constant sadness just to name a few. The beautiful thing about the process of addressing these unresolved issues is that it's very effective whether the perpetuator of your emotional pain is dead or alive. It's not about them. It's about you. Remember, you are working on yourself, so you don't need to ever speak to that person about your pain. You work on it all alone, using this book or with the help of your Grief Recovery specialist or a trusted friend.

THE COMPLETION LETTER

In Grief Recovery, the completion letter is all about putting on paper the said and/or the unsaid. The things you wish you'd said or done differently. It's about giving your pains a voice and letting them speak. Remember, speaking is therapeutic. That's why when you go for counseling or group support, the role of the counselor or group leader isn't to tell you what to do but to give you the opportunity to talk. They may ask some probing questions or make statements to get you to think deeper and come up with some possible choices and answers.

The completion letter has three components:

- Apologies—anything you think you did that may have triggered a negative reaction for which you want to apologize.
- Forgiveness—anything the person did to you that causes you to hold resentment and grudges.
- Significant Emotional Statement—anything worthwhile the person did for you for which you want to register your words of appreciation, or anything you wish the person had done but failed to do on which you wish to make a significant emotional statement.

It's all about telling the person who might be at the root cause of your emotional pain how you feel. You're not concerned about the person's feeling and reaction to what you have to say. In fact, you don't even need to speak to the person, so there's no need to be concerned about their opinion, because chances are that if you were to talk to them about it, you'd be hurt again. If the person has attended Grief Recovery sessions, they'll have a different disposition to you talking to them about your hurt. But in the absence of that, you just want to address your own healing and wellness. All you're concerned about now is your ability to speak by expressing your thoughts on paper.

Having laid the foundation for you, I suggest that at the end of this chapter, in the "Action Step," you take the time to address the unresolved issues in your life, one issue at a time. Since most of our issues involve someone else or self, do your completion letter by addressing one person at a time.

Just think of it like writing a letter or an email. Don't be concerned about style, grammar, or the length of the letter. Just write. While we usually recommend using ink and paper, use whatever works best for you. However, using ink and paper makes it very personal. Do what's best and what works for you, though! There's no right or wrong way when writing the Completion Letter.

While writing your completion letter, it's important to note that you may have some emotional reactions. This is normal. Remember, when the heart is hurting, this is the best way it bleeds out its stored and unresolved emotions. Allow the tears to flow. This is very therapeutic. Don't suppress your emotions. If you do, it's like storing an explosive substance in a bottle and then covering it; at some point, it will explode. Allowing your tears to flow is one of the ways you allow your broken heart to express stored unresolved emotions.

READING YOUR COMPLETION LETTER ALOUD

Reading your completion letter is as important as writing it because you're now about to bring an end to the emotional pain associated with that relationship. Please bear in mind that this won't happen overnight. It may take repeated efforts to make it happen, depending on the depth of your emotional wounds.

I suggest that you find a safe place free of distraction. Sit down and pretend that the person to whom you wrote the letter is in front of you. This implies that you're bringing completion to a relationship *that ended* by way of death, divorce, separation, betrayal, and the list goes on.

> Don't suppress your emotions. If you do, it's like storing an explosive substance in a bottle and then covering it; at some point, it will explode. Allowing your tears to flow is one of the ways you will allow your broken heart to express stored unresolved emotions.

Reading the completion letter is just as important as writing it, so you need to read it aloud. Ensure that you read it in a safe environment. This can be to a trusted friend, in your bathroom alone, in your car, or in a park. In fact, pretend that I'm in front of you and read it to me! Or, in your mind's eye pretend that you're engaging in a monologue, and the person who hurts you is sitting on an empty chair and listening to you, with no ability to interrupt. As you read, remember that your completion letter is all about you bringing completion to the pain caused by the unresolved grief.

In Grief Recovery support sessions, the grievers usually read their letter to me, knowing that I'd never divulge information, as we commit to confidentiality. Furthermore, many of the people I support in grief sessions of any kind are spread across North America, most of whom I've never met in person but only via the telephone or Zoom.

I also ask them to keep this method of working on the deep-seated emotional issues of their lives handy so that they can always use it to heal themselves in the future. It's like a tool; they use it whenever and however they need it. I'm suggesting the same thing to you. Never run away from your problems. If you do, you'll be running for the rest of your life. Address them and bring them to a resolved state of mind.

If you need to read your completion letter to a trusted friend, be sure that you've known your friend long enough to be certain that they won't betray you. If in doubt, find a Grief Recovery specialist near you. It will be worth paying for their services to help you in your quest for emotional healing and wellness.

Reading your completion letter shouldn't be difficult because you can choose where and how you do it. As they say, walls have ears, so be sure you're safe to give voice to your pain.

> Never run away from your problems. If you do, you'll be running for the rest of your life. Address them and bring them to a resolved state of mind.

I don't want you to read this book as a novel but as a step-by-step guide to emotional healing and wellness. I want you to take your time and go through it, taking the necessary steps to address the unresolved issues in your life, in accordance with the suggestion of each chapter.

Once you've completed your recovery letter, evaluate your feelings by asking the following questions:

- How do I feel now, having written and read my completion letter?
- Do I feel a sense of relief?
- Do I feel that the emotional load is getting lighter? ⌐
- Do I feel that I have granted forgiveness to the perpetuator? ‒
- Do I feel that I have forgiven myself? ‒
- Do I feel that I am recovering from the emotional pain? ⌐

Keep working on this until you're totally free from your emotional pain, and take care of your emotional health. I am super proud of you! You must be proud of yourself as well.

Oct 19

CHAPTER SUMMARY AND ACTION STEP

In this chapter, we looked at assessing the present. This section wasn't intended to harm you but to arm you. The future is created based on the decisions of the present. If you need to create a bright future, you can't run away from the reality of the present.

Life will always be challenging. As long as you have the breath of life within you, you will never be exempt from the hurts. Some of the hurts are caused by people who are also hurting but either refuse to address their issues or don't know that help is available; therefore, not knowing how to deal with their hurts, they use the STERBs—the Short-Term Energy Relieving Behaviors to survive and get by.

Children can be victims as well, and unless they're taught how to address their own issues, they too will hurt others, because that's all they know. This vicious cycle will continue until we realize that we're all hurting and need to address our unresolved issues in a proper manner to stop the cycle. This will contribute to making this world a better place.

This is true for most relationships. We can't control people's actions, but we can control our reactions to their actions. Therefore, you must arm yourself with the right attitude to protect yourself from the things you can't control and maintain a high degree of happiness regardless of life's struggles. No one can make you unhappy unless you give them permission. Therefore, the responsibility of being happy and remaining happy must be your sole task.

In life, bad things will happen to you, but you must predispose yourself to forgive. Who do you need to forgive to emancipate yourself from unresolved emotional pain? Identify each person by name, and address each by the magnitude of the pain. Which memory brings to your heart the most pain? Start with that person's name and continue with the next person. This will help you tremendously. Remember why you need to forgive that person. It has nothing to do with him or her. It's all about you and for your own good! It's for your benefit.

Note

STEP 3:
TAKING OWNERSHIP
OF YOUR FUTURE

*True happiness is an inside job cultivated
on the soil of self-worth. It flourishes in an
environment of mutual respect and affection.*
—Emile Maxi

I'VE BEEN A MARRIAGE officer for about thirty years at
the time of writing this book. I've performed many weddings
and conducted lots of pre-marital and post-marital counseling. I've never counseled a couple or performed the wedding
of a couple that got married with the plan to get divorced. Yet
divorces do happen! What happened to Mr. or Mrs. Right?

I can remember the fanfare of the weddings, the expensive
weddings, the glow on their faces, the expensive wedding
bands, the joy and happiness of the moments—only to hear

later the sad news of divorces and the emotional pain that comes with it.

Usually in my pre-marital counseling sessions, the couple goes through an in-depth and rigorous process. They must take a computer-based assessment that involves answering at least 250 questions. The number of sessions is determined by a needs assessment. Based on the graph, it's easy to see the growth areas and the areas that need attention, thus avoiding blind and free-style pre-marital sessions. Yet even after such extensive counseling, the happiness that seemed apparent during the courtship period is all but vanished into thin air a few years after the wedding. This leads one to ask the question: What's the problem?

HAPPINESS IS AN INSIDE JOB, NOT AN OUTSIDE ONE

Unfortunately, far too often I hear the phrase, "When I'm with him or her, I feel so happy and fulfilled. I can't see a life without him or her by my side." At times I'd also hear: "I wasn't happy until I found him or her."

If you've said these words and are still happily married, I'm very happy for you. But I'd also suggest that before you can be happy in a relationship, you must first be happy with yourself. Far too often we look for love to come from the outside only to be utterly disappointed. True happiness is an inside job, cultivated on the soil of self-worth. It flourishes in an environment of mutual respect and affection.

Have you ever wondered why there are so many divorces in the world? To answer this question, we must first ask another one: Have two enemies ever decided to get married? I believe your answer is a resounding "no." So why would two persons who were passionately in love, who decided to unite their lives in holy matrimony, and sign the marriage certificate end up fighting in court and paying a hefty sum of money to lawyers to get them out of their wedding vows: "until death do us part?" Why would two persons who were so in love that they decided not only to get married but also to team up to bring children to this world then cause those children to suffer emotionally as the result of the separation of their parents?

Far too often I see people planning their vacation far better than they plan for their lives. You're probably reading this book with tears in your eyes because you are suffering as the result of a broken relationship. This might even lead to financial disaster. You feel used, abused, and overused. Life has been very brutal to you, to the point where you feel stuck. Don't despair! Regardless of how you feel now, I still want you to repeat the life-changing statement we started with: "I am unstoppable!"

> Far too often I see people planning their vacation far better than they plan for their lives.

Remember, this book is designed to be a self-care guide based on my work as a Grief Recovery specialist, life coach, and marriage counselor. You're getting the necessary help to move you out of the rut of life to the point where no one can stop your progress.

I want to instill the truth in your mind that you are priceless. Let no one tell you otherwise. Yes, I know you might be going through stuff that tells you something else. Your self-confidence may be down in the mud because life has been severely brutal to you. Hold on to this book!

Before I can take you through the life coaching aspect, where I'll deal with the issue of the mind, I need to first help you address the issues of the heart. If you're not happy with yourself, no one and nothing else will be able to make you happy. While others can contribute to your happiness, your true happiness doesn't depend solely on them. You may have the right partner, but he or she won't be able to provide lasting happiness. You may be financially well-off, but your money won't provide true and lasting happiness. Happiness is a state of mind. It cannot be bought or traded.

> If you are not first of all, happy with yourself, no one else and nothing else will be able to make you happy.

Regardless of how much you've been battered by people and life, you are precious. There is gold in you. Emerge from the rubbles of life and shine. Your self-worth isn't based on someone else giving you that worth. It's based on an inherent value. God created only one of you. There is no one else like you on this planet. You are not cheap. You are priceless.

Allow no one to devalue your worth, and don't settle for less than what you are worth. You may have been knocked down, but you're not out. While down, find the courage to look within and see the beauty in you; survey your landscape and take note of the things you need to do to rise and shine. You'll find that when you're happy from within, you'll be able to sift through your potential friends, and if they themselves are happy, it will create an environment in which you can grow based on mutual respect and affection. You deserve the best, so don't settle for less.

To help you take ownership of your true sense of happiness, let me lead you to reflect on this subject by asking you to write your own definition of happiness. Whatever your definition might be, it is unique to you. For each one of us, it has its own meaning and looks different. You don't want to be like the "Jones" because you don't know what they did to be where they are. In fact, it may end up being just an appearance.

> You are not cheap. You are priceless. Allow no one to devalue your worth. Don't settle for less than what you are worth.

Regardless of your circumstances, there is one very important truth I want you to always bear in mind. You must take some level of responsibility for how you allow your circumstances to affect your happiness. While it's true that happiness is an inside job, people can contribute to your happiness, but no one can make you unhappy without your permission.

CHANGE YOUR ATTITUDE, CHANGE YOUR WORLD

You know yourself better than anyone else, so for you to be happy, you ought to know what makes you happy and what makes you sad and create your own bubble. You need to know your environment. As I reflected on my own life, I concluded that there were three kinds of people in our lives: the left-behinds, the relays, and the anchors.

- **The First Group of People.** I call this group the "left-behinds." These are the people who come into our lives and aren't meant to stay for long. They have a specific assignment to teach us something, whether good or bad, but eventually we have to move on and leave them behind. They were never meant to stay. When we think of them, once they're gone, it either brings us pain or pleasure. Regardless of the memory, it was worth it. They came into our lives to give us a push so that we could go a bit further in our journey of life—our race. If we acknowledge this fact, even when the memories are painful, we'll accept it as a fact of life, hence we shouldn't lament over their departure or allow it to control our mood and destiny. They came and did what was meant to be. We accept it for what it was worth, and we move on!

- **The Second Group of People.** I call this group the "relays." A relay race in athletics is an event whereby a team of athletes run equal predetermined distances in a sprint race. Each athlete has a specific duty, which is to run and take the baton to the next athlete, who in turn will take it to the next, until the last person successfully grabs the baton and crosses the finish line to victory. The final runner is called the "anchor." The relays come into our lives with the specific purpose to take us further than the ones we left behind. These are chosen based on their level of strength, endurance, and stamina. We need these kinds of people in our lives, as they're the ones who will help us get closer to our goals and objectives. We need to identify them as we go through the race of life. They will help us tremendously to be stronger. Don't neglect their purpose in your life. The closer we are to them, the more we'll be influenced by them to get closer to the finish line.

- **The Third Group of People.** I call this group the "anchors." The last runner in a relay race is called the "anchor," chosen because of some specific characteristics. They are swifter. They are lighter. They have more endurance. They are very focused. They have a winning attitude. When these people come into your life, they want to make you successful, to mentor you, to coach you, and to cheer you on to victory. Because they have run the race, they know what it's like to coach you to run your race. If allowed, they'll coach to your victory. It's important to find them and stay close to them and make them your anchors.

Life is a race, but we can't win life's race alone. One is too small of a number to achieve anything worthwhile in life. You need to take advantage of all three groups mentioned above. Life is far too complex, so it requires a team to win the race. It's very easy to downplay the place of each runner in the relay when we win, but don't make that mistake! There's no failure in life if we can learn something from it. Regardless of how bad the experience, try to learn from it.

You are who you are today not just because of the good people you met but also because of the bad ones. In fact, the bad ones contribute to your fortitude far more than you can appreciate.

> One is too small of a number to achieve anything worthwhile in life.

At times you wished you could change your circumstances. Although you can't change your external world, you can change your internal world. John C. Maxwell in his book *Developing the Leader within You* says, "everything falls and rises on leadership."[1] It's largely due to the attitude of the leader. I find that when I change my attitude towards people or life, everything looks different.

To illustrate this, I'm going to use myself as an example. There was a time when I didn't wear eyeglasses. Without the eyeglasses, I could see the world clearly from a distance.

As times went by and I got older, I went to school one day and realized that I couldn't see the chalkboard. Everything was blurry to me. When I reported that to my siblings, I was taken to an ophthalmologist and then to an optometrist. My eyesight was very bad, so, I was prescribed eyeglasses. When I went to school with my eyeglasses, everything was crystal clear! What happened? What changed? My eyesight or my classroom? No, it wasn't my classroom. Everything in my classroom remained the same. My eyesight changed. The eyeglasses allowed me to see everything differently. This is what I'd like for you. Change your attitude and you change your world. Everything rises and falls on attitude!

As we come to the end of this chapter, I want you to take a moment to reflect on the past. Life has been brutal to you. You can't move into the future with your past hurts. You need to lighten your heart of all this emotional baggage. Let it go! There's far too much great stuff in store for you in the future. Let it go so that you can enjoy life!

Embark on the things that are meaningful to you and give you a greater sense of purpose. Know what contributes to your happiness and pursue them! Focus on these things. Work on these things. Be a part of something that elevates you and others. Make it your point of duty to find your new niche, and associate with those who elevate you and help you reach your full potential. Avoid people who specialize in tearing you down. Find your anchor and thrive!

CONTRIBUTING TO A WIDER CAUSE

One of the things that makes a big different in my life is my ability to take a keen interest in the lives and the welfare of others. As I grow older and observe successful and happy people, it seems clear to me that the ones who are the happiest are the ones who are altruistic. They seem to be passionate about helping others.

They don't do it to gain recognition or fame. In fact, most of the time they don't even want to be acknowledged for their involvement in the welfare of others. If their names or their deeds are mentioned, it's not because they blew their own trumpet but because the recipient of their kindness wants to show gratitude. If you do something for someone and are looking for praise and recognition, check yourself and your motives.

Over the years, we've heard of firefighters who saved others by risking their lives. We've heard of people who saved total strangers from drowning, or of police officers risking their own lives to save or rescue others from a mass shooting. We've heard of people who share a loaf of bread with someone who doesn't have anything to eat, or people who volunteer at a local charity to help serve the less fortunate. We've heard of people who retire for the sole purpose of having more time to help others. The contributions of many people who receive Nobel prizes are unknown until it's made public. Why do people do these things? Most of the time, it's not to gain recognition or become heroes. Their hearts just propelled them to do what needed to be done, and someone was grateful for it and recognized them.

If you do anything for anyone with ulterior motives, or to show off, you ultimately become a manipulator, and eventually you'll be the most unhappy person in this life.

> If you do anything for anyone with ulterior motives, or to show off, you ultimately become a manipulator, and eventually you'll be the most unhappy person in this life.

WORKING ON GOD'S EXPECTATIONS OF YOU

Unselfishly helping others is one of the greatest gifts you can give to your community and to yourself. I've been working as a pastor for thirty years, which involves helping others with their varying needs. I wouldn't trade it for a million dollars. But if I could keep the million, it would go towards helping more people. Why? It gives me something money can't buy. If you have money, you can use it to transform lives and fulfill God's expectations of you. Similarly, if you don't have a dollar to your name, yet you can find it in your heart to help others, you too would have changed God's expectations of you. God clearly stated this in Isaiah 1:11–17. If you read this chapter, it will change your view of religiosity. When I read this passage, it totally changed my worldview. The way I practice my Christianity today is far different from the way I did some years ago.

Do you now understand why it has changed my worldview? What has it done for you? Religion is meaningless without the application of Isaiah 1:17: "learn to do good; seek justice, correct oppression; bring justice to the fatherless, plead the widow's cause."[2]

This is the test of any true religion. Go and fulfill your God-given responsibilities. Seek justice for the underprivileged, and help the oppressed. Defend the cause of the orphans. Fight for the rights of widows. Set your heart right with God's expectations of you. Your heart will be merry! This may be the beginning of your happiness.

CHAPTER SUMMARY AND ACTION STEP

Your happiness should be your number one priority. Anything that takes away your happiness should be avoided at all costs. If you're not happy, it will eventually affect the quality of your life and your health. Is it worth it?

True happiness is an inside job, cultivated in the soil of self-worth. It flourishes in an environment of mutual respect and mutual affection. Happiness isn't just about making yourself happy but also how you can contribute to the happiness of others.

To ensure your own happiness, you need to ask yourself the following questions:

- Are you happy with your current situation and life as a whole?
- What do you need to change to ensure your own happiness?
- When are you going to start doing what you need to do to change?
- Who is affecting your sense of happiness?
- How can you best address this situation to ensure that they don't steal your joy and happiness?
- What are the things that contribute to your happiness?
- How are you going to maximize on the things that bring you joy and happiness to ensure you're not just living but are thriving?
- Who can you rely on to help you in this process?

- Who is your "left-behinds," your "relays," and your "anchors"?
- What have they done for you for which you are grateful?
- What role can you play in the life of someone else to help them get a notch closer to their goal?
- Can you identify a few persons in your circle whom you can mentor and contribute to their happiness?
- When are you going to start mentoring these persons?

STEP 4:
FACING THE GIANT IN YOU

There is a giant within you. It can either make
you or break you. It's all your choice.
—Emile Maxi

THERE'S A FASCINATING STORY in the Bible that's worth mentioning as we look at the giants within us. It's about David and Goliath and is recorded in 1 Samuel 17. The Israelites were paralyzed by even the mention of the word "Philistines." This was one of the most powerful nations on earth at that time. They had defeated Israel several times in battle. They were known as a fearless nation. Let me highlight and paraphrase Goliath's characteristics as described in the New Living Translation (NLT):

- He was the champion from Gath.
- He was over nine feet tall.

- He wore a bronze helmet.
- His bronze coat of mail weighed 125 pounds.
- He also wore bronze leg armor.
- He carried a bronze javelin on his shoulder.
- The shaft of his spear was as heavy and thick as a weaver's beam, tipped with an iron spearhead that weighed 15 pounds.
- His armor bearer walked ahead of him carrying a shield.

Wow! The sight of this champion named Goliath drove fear. He was massive. He was intimidating. Just the sight of him was paralyzing. These were the days when wars used to be fought in close proximity, as modern-day artillery hadn't even been thought of. The army of Israel was no match. They were less equipped. They weren't that tall or as experienced. The sight of Goliath crippled them.

But in the midst of Israel was a teenage boy who had absolutely no life experience or military training. His resume contained only the epithet, "shepherd boy." All he knew was how to care for the sheep of his father and play the harp to keep himself from boredom as he cared for the most naïve, peaceful, and harmless of the animal kingdom.

The commander-in-chief of Israel's army declared David unfit to represent the army of Israel. By all military standards, he was no match to take on Goliath. Even his older brother, Eliab, who was a well-trained soldier, wanted to take on this ferocious, merciless monster-man and was furious at little David. He thought of David as proud, deceitful, and curious. No one in their right mind believed that this conceited teenager really believed that with all the power given to him from "above" he could take on Goliath. He saw how this bloodthirsty "invincible" vampire made the army of Israel run away in fright.

They had been terrified by the sight of Goliath for forty days. They knew this giant had brought down other nations more powerful than them, and they didn't want to take a chance. The King of Israel, the handsome and powerful Saul, was so eager to get rid of Goliath that he promised to give a huge reward to the man who killed him. What? The shepherd boy got even more "bold." Reward!

"What could that be?" he asked.

"One of the king's daughters for a wife," answered a trusted source! Plus, tax exemption for all his family.

"What? Are you kidding me? I'm in," David said convincingly. "I am all in! Yes, I can! Are you serious? I'll pay no taxes, and you mean a girl on top of that? What else? I've been dreaming all my life for a girl, and now I get to have one of the daughters of the king. This was never part of my dream because I'm a realistic and pragmatic dreamer. I know such a dream could never come true for a shepherd boy. But I want that girl—the king's daughter!"

A well -decorated soldier heard his internal reasoning and shouted, "Conceited, you are indeed an 'adult-less-sense!' Oops, I'm sorry, I meant an adolescent."

But this teenage boy was fearless. Word got to King Saul and he heard of the bravery of this shepherd boy. He called him in, and at the sight of him, the King was absolutely convinced that he was too young, too short, too immature, too inexperienced, and too ridiculous to aim so high as killing a well-decorated war expert like Goliath.

"'Don't be ridiculous!' Saul replied. 'There's no way you can fight this Philistine and possibly win! You're only a boy, and he's been a man of war since his youth'" (1 Samuel 17:33, NLT).

These negative words could have demoralized the shepherd boy, but his intrinsic motivation and faith-filled drive gave him the internal courage to believe in himself and that he could bring down the giant.

The shepherd boy didn't have an impressive resume to present, so he had to pull out his private accomplishments to impress the king. He knew that Goliath had to be taken down before he took down the armies of Israel. In fact, morally speaking, he knew that Israel was already down. Morally and emotionally down!

He had to rely on the only thing he possessed to pump them up—a faith-filled drive to win this battle. The army of Israel had two things that he didn't, which were expertise and experience. David, however, had something that they didn't have: the will to succeed, the right attitude to win, and, most of all, a strong faith in the divine power.

To win your battle, you need the same—the will to succeed, the right attitude, and a strong faith in the power that is greater than you.

The shepherd boy got fitted with the king's protective gear and ready for the battle. "No, shouted the teenage boy, "I cannot move in these, Chief!"

After all, he wasn't an army man; he had never used an armor or a coat of mail or a bronze helmet before. They were foreign to his civilian body. These were too fancy, let alone using the king's armor.

> To win your battle, you need the same—the will to succeed, the right attitude, and a strong faith in the power that is greater than you.

All he was accustomed to was the use of little pebble stones and a sling to launch them at his flock to propel straying sheep back into the fold. This became his weapon of war. At the sight of this, even the army of Israel laughed. "Are you insane! What can you do with this? Are you hunting for birds?" they uttered. The Philistines laughed and felt insulted! The shepherd boy was convinced that his weapon was good enough to bring down the nine-feet-tall giant. Before they knew it, this courageous shepherd boy reached out for it in his tattered bag and used it, and now the monster-walking-giant became the nine-feet-long dead soul. Then David did something remarkable: "...he stored the man's (Goliath's) armor in his own tent" (1 Samuel 17:54b, NLT).

Why did he do this? I want to believe it was because David wanted a constant reminder each time the sun's rays hit Goliath's armor that with God all things are possible—if you believe and act in faith.

Goliath's armor could have been heavier than David's body weight, yet David brought him down. What does it tell you about the giants in your life? Can you bring them down? Oh, yes, you can!

WHAT'S YOUR GIANT?

We all have a giant in us or among us. What's yours? Facing the giant in you might be the most important thing you need to do right now to heal yourself. No one can stop you but you!

Let's face the giant within that may cause us to be stuck as a result of our unresolved emotional issues. Once more you need to remind yourself that you are being healed. So may I suggest that you say it again: "I am being healed."

> Facing the giant in you might be the most important thing you need to do right now to heal yourself. No one can stop you but you!

Did you identify the "giant within" that might be holding you back? Different people will have different giants. I will address them one by one, hoping that you're using these tools to address yours. If you don't conquer your giants within, there's a great probability that they will conquer you. I really don't want that for you. Let's identify some of them:

- habits (in this case, bad habits)

- fear
- regrets
- addiction
- low self-esteem
- depression and anxiety
- confusion
- lack of knowledge
- lack of financial and human resources

DEALING WITH HABITS

In your quest to be healed and unstoppable, it's important that you address the bad habits in your life. They might be the giants that are stopping you from reaching your full potential. To get rid of bad habits, you need to develop a system to help you. That system should be something that works best for you and may include some trusted family members and friends to help you become a victor. To ensure that you remain a victor, you must stay away from anyone and/or any place that may pull you back into your bad habits and turn you back into a victim. Strive to be a victor but not a victim.

Even a 10% victory over a bad habit should be considered a gain and must be celebrated. It adds up. That's the power of compounding interest.

> Did you identify the "giant within" that might be holding you back?

I write this book to be a real companion to your success. I don't want you to just read it. I want you to use it as a manual to make you unstoppable. It's all about you, but don't expect to be unstoppable overnight. It will come as the result of your desire to succeed in life. All I know is that it will happen if you're committed and only if you are:

- aware that you're stuck
- having a burning desire to get out of the deep hole
- willing to do whatever it takes to get out of your unpleasant situation
- willing to apply these principles to your life
- in possession of a strong sense of commitment
- willing to create a system that works for you that will enable you to stay away from your bad habits and anybody who may drag you back into them

To help you, here are two questions that you need to answer and address:

- What are the bad habits in your life that you need to conquer?
- What system are you going to put in place to ensure you have victory over your habits? Remember, you need to conquer your bad habits before they conquer you. Don't doubt yourself; you can do it. Bad habits cannot and will not stop you. Why? Because you are unstoppable.

> There might be the giants that are stopping you from reaching your full potential.

DEALING WITH FEAR

Fear. The four-letter word that can paralyze the potential that lies within. If not dealt with, it can be deadly.

- What can stop you? Fear can.
- What can make you unstoppable? Facing and conquering your fear! This is the monster, the giant within that must be conquered.

Fear is so debilitating, so paralyzing, so deadly, that it can steal away big dreams, aspirations, and potential. Fear can paralyze and disarm the most powerful army to the point where they lose their ability to use their own artillery. Fear can produce more than enough adrenaline to cause us to take our flight or to fight.

When thinking of fear, no other speech moves me more than the inaugural speech of President Franklin D. Roosevelt. Because of my love for history and great speeches, whenever I'm reading a book and the writer only mentions a few lines of the speech, I get so disappointed. Thinking that you and I might share the same sentiment, I would suggest that you read President Roosevelt's entire speech for your perusal. Please refer to note #3 at the end of the book under chapter 4. I don't want you to just read his speech but to analyze it. I want to move you into action, do not allow fear to cripple you. We can't expect to be healed and be unstoppable unless we deal with the fear in our lives.

I would recommend that you read FDR's inaugural presidential address and I want you to determine what he was trying to achieve when he mentioned the term "fear." What was he trying to accomplish? He used fear in different forms to inspire the nation to stand firm in the face of great adversity. In his speech, he says: "The only thing we have to fear is fear itself."[3]

What was FDR trying to dissipate in the minds of the American people? The straight answer is fear. What has it done for you? For me it's a life-changer. FDR's inaugural address gives me what I need the most—the dissipation of fear in me. I am not an American, but his speech knows no boundary and no citizenship. It helps me to be fearless.

Remember the context of FDR's inaugural speech. The year 1933 was one of great political crisis. War and the talk of war were looming. With that came adversity, uncertainty, and scarcity. The American people needed hope. They needed reassurance. They needed a sense of direction in the face of adversity. They needed to hear these words of encouragement that breathed life into them. At a time such as this, FDR said: "The only thing we have to fear is fear itself."[3]

I want the words of President Roosevelt to echo in your ears until they move you to action.

Fear. At some point we all experience it, but it must not consume us. So what do we do? Here is an effective way I address my fear:

- First, I acknowledge the fact that I am fearful. There's nothing wrong in that. We may or may not necessarily show it externally, but it's important to acknowledge that it's present within us. This is the first step towards healing. Acknowledge my fear. We're not always as bold as David in facing our giant.

- Second, I want to know what's at the root of my fear. In order words, I want to know what causes me to be afraid. This allows me to investigate the basis of my fear. Is it lack of information? Is it fear of the unknown? Is it fear of losing money or of losing face? Is it the fear of losing trust? The list goes on.

- Third, I must muster the courage to face my fear and conquer it once and for all. Far too often, we allow our fear to cripple our ability to take chances. I heard someone once said, "If we are afraid to lose, we will never win." This is so true! While fear is a natural response to something unfamiliar and scary, we can't afford to live in fear, or else we'll always be dominated by it and its sources, whether it's a person, the unknown, or an object. It's imperative that we conquer our fear, or it will conquer us.

As you take the necessary steps to take back full control of your life, take control of your fear before it takes control of you. President FDR's inaugural speech did wonders for the American people. It did wonders for me. I hope it will do the same for you.

THE REGRETS

> While fear is a natural response to something that is
> unfamiliar and scary, we can't afford to live in fear, or
> else we'll always be dominated by it and its sources,
> whether it's a person, the unknown, or an object. It's
> imperative that we conquer our fear, or it will conquer us.

This is another word that can prevent us from developing our full potential. What is regret? Well, you can define it as fast as anyone else. You've certainly had many regrets in your life.

Regrets are all about the feeling of sadness and disappointment over the things we said or did, or over the things we wish we could have done or said differently. It's normal to have regrets, but it's not helpful to dwell on them. Why? We cannot change the past. Yes, we regret the hurts caused by what was said or done. Things could have been different. But you can learn from your regrets so that you do better in the future. Don't let them dominate your life and ruin your future.

ADDICTIONS

Far too often, our regrets lead us into addictions. These can be addictions of any kind. Unfortunately, the consequences of our addictions can be severe. These addictions not only affect us but also our loved ones. Their consequences can even extend to many generations as their damaging effects are passed on. They deeply affect our relationships and our ability to thrive. They often lead to separation, divorce, bankruptcy, and verbal, sexual, emotional, and physical abuse. They can even lead to death. Unfortunately, innocent children are the ones who are affected the most. They, in turn, continue this vicious cycle of addiction and ultimately become abusive also.

Acknowledging that you're addicted to something is the right step into the path of healing. There is no healing until you acknowledge your addiction and seek appropriate help. Plenty of agencies exist to offer help and support. The problem of addition is not a "his or her problem" but "our problem." It's a problem that all of us must be involved in solving.

> Acknowledging that you're addicted to something is the right step into the path of healing. There is no healing until you acknowledge your addiction and seek appropriate help.

Acknowledgment is the key. If you're not addicted, you can help those who are addicted to seek professional help. Seeking help is a sign of strength. So for your own sake and that of your loved ones, you owe it to yourself to get back on track. Remember, you are being healed and you are unstoppable. Relying on illicit drugs is not the way to heal yourself from emotional pain. Regardless of your varying types of unresolved emotional issues, seek the appropriate help! There is help for you!

- If it's a marital issue, most pastors are equipped to offer marital counseling, and most of the times they offer free services as a service of the church to the community. If they do charge, it's usually far cheaper than seeing a private counselor.

- If it's a matter of unresolved grief due to relationship issues, separation, divorce, death of a loved one, pet loss, loss of trust, moving, loss of health, or forgiveness issues, seek the help of a Grief Recovery specialist. Some pastors, like myself, offer this kind of service based on our additional training in this field. They will be happy to help address your unresolved issues. In addition to pastors, other people offer this service on a full-time basis for a living. They will be happy to help you for a modest remuneration. You can visit the Grief Recovery Institute website, of which I'm a part. You can enter your city and search for a Grief Recovery specialist near you. The website is https://www.griefrecoverymethod.com.

- If it's a matter of addiction to alcohol, you can visit an Alcoholics Anonymous near you. Their website is: https://www.aa.org.

- If it's a matter of any other form of addiction, or for general information, you can visit: https://www.healthline.com/health/addiction/recognizing-addiction.

LOW SELF-ESTEEM

Low self-esteem can have many and varied causes. It's very common among those who have been abused physically, verbally, psychologically, mentally, and emotionally. This is worsened especially when it happens over a period of time without being addressed.

Unfortunately, it can also manifest itself from childhood experiences based on how a child was treated by their parents, caregivers, or siblings. If not addressed, it can lead to social issues and the inability to express oneself. It can also seriously affect their level of assertiveness. This, however, is not all doom and gloom. Where there's a will, there's a way. With proper help from a trained professional and the determination on the part of the person, it can be addressed and resolved.

In marital counseling sessions, I have far too often seen the devastating effects of low self-esteem in romantic relationship, especially among women. It's always heartbreaking to see a person who is well educated, well accomplished, and used to be full of confidence be brought down to low self-esteem as the result of the degrading words of a spouse. This low self-esteem has the potential to make one feel so worthless that it even affects their ability to look at you and speak their mind in a rational and confident way. At times, such a person ends up searching for love to regain their sense of self-worth through a relationship and sadly gets hurt again and again.

> This low self-esteem has the potential to make one feel so worthless that it even affects their ability to look at you and speak their mind in a rational and confident way.

If you find yourself in this category, it's advisable that you spend some time addressing the unresolved issues in your life and work hard to build yourself back before you get back into a relationship. At such a time, you are so vulnerable, you tend to fall for any man that is good with his words and says what you really want to hear to sweep you off your feet only to get hurt again. I'm not suggesting that you won't find the right man, but if you decide to give it a try, you need to tread softly. You need to be as wise as a serpent. Surround yourself with family and friends who love you so much that they're prepared to tell you the hardest truth but in a loving way to help you stay on track lest you end up with another villain.

> At such a time, you are so vulnerable, you tend to fall for any man that is good with his words and says what you really want to hear to sweep you off your feet only to get hurt again.

If you're going to be healed, you need to keep your eyes fixed on the prize, which is emotional health. Getting into the right relationship at the wrong time can also be devastating because you may have the right person, but if you're not emotionally in the right heart space and head space, chances are you're going to hurt each other and ruin something that could have been great had you given yourself a few months to get all your emotional ducks in the right rows. If he loves you that much, he can wait until the right time to get involved in a romantic relationship. Never underestimate the power of proper counseling sessions. If you've never been hurt in a romantic relationship, and you're seriously courting, you owe it to yourself to get counseling. If you've been hurt before, you need to be even more vigilant.

> If you are going to be healed, you need to keep your eyes fixed on the prize, which is emotional health. Getting into the right relationship at the wrong time can also be devastating.

Too many emotional blows caused by several break-ups can be very damaging. You need to protect yourself and your future. Far too often I see women develop dislike or even hatred for men because of their past hurts by other males. They seem to suggest that if they're not careful, they might end up in other rounds of hurts. If as the result of some bad relationships you treat all men as equal villains, you might end up with one of those villains if you're not careful. Even in your hurts you need to always maintain a positive attitude. By being positive, you're also attracted to positive people. So keep the negative out of your mind. Your lips shouldn't even annunciate it. Similarly, women who have been in abusive relationships tend to end up in the hands of men who are abusive. Why? I leave you to do the research and stay away from the losers.

If you've been abused or are dealing with low self-esteem, I want you to know that you are worthy of God's love. He wants to turn your sorrow in to joy, if you let Him.

> Even in your hurts, you need to always maintain a positive attitude. By being positive, you're also attracted to positive people. So keep the negative out of your mind. Your lips shouldn't even annunciate it.

You may be asking yourself the question: How can I regain the confidence I once had? The answer lies within your own power. You have the power to change that. Far too often, people allow themselves to be abused by their partner and don't want to talk about it, let alone seek appropriate help. Sometimes they chose to suffer for the sake of their children or because they don't have the means to provide for themselves if they end the relationship and move out.

Again, it goes back to fear. This can keep you from moving ahead. It can keep you from the emotional healing you so desire, but it doesn't mean you can't be healed. You need to take that bold step towards your emotional healing. It's solely your responsibility.

There is so much help available to you. There are lots of kind people in this world, more than you can fathom. To get unstuck, don't be afraid to call your local church or your local women's center to see what programs they have available to help you.

> You need to take that bold step towards your emotional healing. It's solely your responsibility.

Most churches and women's centers offer counseling sessions for people like you. Refuse to allow anyone to treat you less than you deserve. You deserve the best, and if that person isn't treating you with love, respect, and admiration, they don't deserve you. While the abuser needs to have proper counseling sessions to help them address the issues in their life, if for any reason you choose to stay in that relationship, you need to seek help for both of you. If they feel they don't need counseling, then it might be time for you to make your decision. It's not my job to tell you what to do, but you know what you must do to free yourself of emotional pains.

When deciding, it's extremely important to think of your own wellbeing. The longer you stay in an abusive relationship, the worse it gets. Unfortunately, if children are involved and they watch this unfold right before them, chances are they too might be scarred for life. You have the power to stop the cycle with you. You can be healed if you take the right measures.

ANXIETY AND DEPRESSION

While the purpose of this book is not to address mental illness, I will briefly make mention of it here to bring awareness so that I can encourage you to seek professional help.

Only people who are trained to deal with mental illness should be consulted. I don't have any credential in this field, so I won't mislead you. If you're a religious person, while prayer may be a very important part of your faith and belief, this should not replace the help of a mental health professional. Failing to do so may drive you into a deeper state of depression.

Many factors can cause depression, so getting a proper assessment is key to healing. Remember, you are the first and best doctor of your body. You know how you feel. You know what's not right. You can sense it. Seek professional help.

This is why your health professional always asks you about your issues before they can diagnose and treat you. Without that information, they can't do anything. Depending on what's going on in your life, you may know the cause of your anxiety and depression. If you know the cause, it makes it easier to be treated. Do not delay!

In my line of work as a church pastor, marriage counselor, Grief Recovery specialist, and life coach, I often see people go into depression for several reasons, like:

- losing a loved one by death
- losing a job
- news about a terminal illness
- divorce and separation

While I'm not a mental health specialist, I have found that when I pay a pastoral visit to a parishioner who has fallen into one of the four categories mentioned above and is in a depression, their symptoms are usually obvious. Very often, they report no known history of mental issues, except for their feeling of a deep sense of grief. That's why in Grief Recovery support we find the symptoms of grief and depression are very similar. If it's indeed grief related, we attempt to deal with it, but if it's depression in the truest sense of the term, we refer the person to a mental health specialist.

You may wonder how a person who is experiencing grief from these events can be healed. It all boils down to their attitude, their willingness and determination to not just survive but thrive. Arm yourself with the will power, determination, and the right attitude, and you'll be emotionally healed—no question about it!

CONFUSION

When life is brutally difficult, what's needed to free the mind of any sense of confusion? The answer is clarity of mind. When the mind is foggy, we become impaired and unable to make rational decisions. Far too often when we don't possess clarity of mind and a sound spirit, we tend to make more mistakes.

I often see this level of confusion when I accompany a parishioner to the funeral home to make funeral arrangements for their loved ones, or when I'm counseling a person who is fighting a nasty divorce, or when I'm in life coach or Grief Recovery sessions with someone who's dealing with deep emotional issues, or when I'm comforting someone who just got bad news about a life-threatening illness. Quite often, these people are in desperation. "Pastor, please tell me what to do," they'll say. This obviously is a typical sign of mental exhaustion and confusion. In my thirty years of working with and helping people, when that happens, they often say what I don't like to hear: "Oh, I feel like driving myself under a bus or a train," or, "I feel like ending my life."

A confused mind can deprive us of the ability to articulate our thoughts and feelings, and we become desperate. When that happens, we don't even know where to turn for help. If surrounded by dependable and trusted relatives and friends, they literally may have to take their hands and guide them to the appropriate help to health and wellness.

How can someone with a confused mind find help and move from being emotionally drained to emotional health? The answer is simple: they must have trusted family and friends on whose strong shoulders they can lean. This is where belonging to a community of caring people matters. Do you have such a support? Or can you be that support to someone in need? When this happens, it's important that you deal with the person with a deep sense of trust and loyalty, honesty, ethics, and respect.

You might be well physically, but the emotional aspects might take a hit by life's brutality, hence you need some guidance. We all need a little of that from time to time. As you read this book, if you find yourself experiencing confusion, or you know you have lots of ideas but feel stuck, here are some questions to ask yourself:

- Why do I feel this way?
- What is the root cause of my confusion?
- What are the many thoughts racing through my brain?
- Which of my many racing thoughts do I want to deal with first?

- What is the main thought that I need to focus on and deal with?
- Which should be given top priority in order of importance?
- Who can help me address these priorities?
- What additional information do I need to effectively address these concerns?
- Who can I rely on to accompany me through this process?
- How will this process help me?
- How will I feel at the end of the process?
- How long will it take to accomplish this process?
- What will be the desired outcome?
- How will I feel at the end of this process?
- How and to whom will I show gratitude at the end of this process?

LACK OF KNOWLEDGE

Quite often, people are confused and overwhelmed simply because they don't know what to do or the first step to get themselves unstuck. This creates emotional reactions. They don't realize that the world is filled with wonderful people who are willing to help; they only need to ask and keep asking the right people the right questions.

Today, the internet shrinks this huge universe and places it in the palm of our hands—a Smartphone. Knowledge is only a keystroke away. This will be discussed at length when we get to the life coach aspect of my journey with you. The sense of feeling stuck is only temporary if we're willing to make use of modern technology and kind-hearted people to help us move forward. Whatever emotional issues you may be having, you can simply do a Google search and it will guide you to the appropriate office. I'm not suggesting that you rely on the internet blindly. There are lots of dishonest people there too. You'll need to be prudent and not afraid to share your search with a trusted friend or younger person who might help you vet it all—just to be sure you're not misled.

LACK OF FINANCIAL AND HUMAN RESOURCES

The lack of financial and human resources should never be a deterrent in our quest for emotional health and wellness. Where there's a will, there's a way. You need to address this and get well. This is an investment in yourself. If you're passionate about achieving something, once you have the right attitude, the right approach, and you believe in it, you will attract the right people with the financial and technical abilities you need to make it happen. There are lots of people who want you to get well. They will invest in you if they see that you're determined to get better. You shouldn't be ashamed of not being emotionally well. You have a lot to contribute to society. This shouldn't stop you from achieving your dreams. Take care of yourself. Invest in yourself!

I needed to address your emotional issues first before taking you to the next level, which is the life coach aspect. This way, from a Grief Recovery point of view, I can help you clean up the cobweb in the heart to make space for the things that will make you unstoppable—the symbiotic relationship between the heart and the mind. When one has unresolved emotional issues, the cognitive mind doesn't function well. I hope this provided some help.

You have come so far in the process, and for this you have earned another badge of honor. I am very proud of you. Be proud of yourself too! Let's move forward!

> You have a lot to contribute to society. Take care of yourself. Invest in yourself!

CHAPTER SUMMARY AND ACTION STEP

We all have our internal giant that haunts us. For the children of Israel, it was Goliath. What is the giant keeping you awake at night? We can't keep running away from the giants in our lives. We must face them and deal with them once and for all. The Bible says: "For God has not given us a spirit of fear and timidity, but of power, love and self-discipline" (2 Timothy 1:7, NLT).

I'm inviting you to use that power of love and self-discipline to free yourself from anything keeping you from being emotionally free. You have suffered far too long to continue living in fear. You were created to enjoy life to the fullest. If you're not, you owe it to yourself to investigate the different areas of your life and address them one at a time and once and for all.

It's important that you take the time to develop your action plan as to how you're going to address the giants in your life so that you can start your journey to emotional healing and wellness.

1. Can you identify your giants? Write them down and take the necessary actions.

    1.

    2.

    3.

    4.

    5.

Don't grieve continually.

2. How are you going to address them?
   1.
   2.
   3.
   4.
   5. *Let God help me.*

3. Who will you rely on to help you address them?
   1.
   2.
   3.
   4.
   5.
   This book.

4. Do you need professional help to assist you in addressing the giants in your life that are keeping you from achieving emotional health?

   Yes:

   No:

   Not Sure:
   Have my journal.

5. When will you start addressing them?
   Already have.

STEP 5:
SETTING YOURSELF FREE

*Freedom is a state of the mind. You cannot
live it until the mind experiences it.*

—Emile Maxi

YOU HAVE BEEN LET down—not once, not twice, but
countless times. It hurts, and it hurts badly. It leaves you
devastated. You've come to the place where you're afraid to
trust because you can't afford to allow yourself to get hurt
again. This may have come from sweet and loving relationships that went bitterly brutal and sorrowful. You may be
fighting a court case that is draining you mentally, physically,
emotionally, and financially. You don't know where to turn.
Everything seems to be against you. Don't lose hope! This
is the sole purpose of this book! To help you regain what
seemed to have been lost.

The person you thought had your back ended up back-stabbing you. That's the straw that broke the camel's back. You're in a delusion and bewildered. You look at the mirror and wonder if the person you see is the same one you knew years ago. You look worn out. You look like you could do with a little facelift. Who can give you that facelift? you ask. I know someone who can give you that facelift. His name is Jesus. He gave me and others that facelift many times over, but you must want that facelift.

As you reflect on yourself, you notice that you've always poured yourself out to improve the lives of others. These may include your spouse, your children, your relatives, your co-workers, your friends. Often, you're taken advantage of.

You've given so much, but you don't get the same treatment in return, and it tears you apart. Not to mention the ill-treatment and the betrayal. Because of your personality, it's almost like a sin to invest quality time in yourself. The time has come for you to be a bit selfish. To invest in yourself. Do the things you must do—not for someone else but for you. I suggest that you stop blaming yourself for the things that went wrong in your life.

FORGIVE YOURSELF

While we wish we had made better choices in life to avoid these heartaches we're now experiencing, unfortunately, we weren't born with wisdom. We acquire wisdom based on past mistakes. But the acquisition of wisdom doesn't mean we won't slip again. We don't know the human heart. Most often the ones we trust end up being the ones that let us down. Quite often, we even mess up too! This can bring feelings of guilt and moments of sleeplessness. We're so sorry for the things we did or didn't do, and the things we said or didn't say. At times, we're even afraid to apologize because we're afraid of making ourselves vulnerable or being misunderstood.

Before you can forgive others, you first must forgive yourself. This is the first step towards emotional health and wellness. If you're not a person of faith, I'm not trying to convert you. Rather, I'm trying to help you heal your emotional wound. Regardless of what you're blaming yourself for, I want you to know that your heavenly Father forgives you. He knows your good intentions; He knows your heart. He knows your limitations.

> Before you can forgive others, you first must forgive yourself.

He knows you more than you know yourself. He even knows your motives. You are worn down by life and its brutality. Do not give up! Your heavenly Father wants to give you what no one else can give you—the peace that passes all understanding. But for that to happen, you must free yourself from the sense of guilt. We all make mistakes. Blaming yourself will get you nowhere. God wants to get you somewhere, but it can't happen until you forgive yourself. Talking to God about the things you're sorry for is the only and best medicine for the disease of guilt. I pray to God daily and ask

Him daily to forgive me of my shortcomings. I would invite you to do same.

This is something no one can do for you. Asking God for forgiveness is a personal responsibility. And when we ask God for forgiveness, we must believe that it is granted. You and I can take comfort in these words from the Bible: "If we confess our sins, he is faithful and just and will forgive us our sins and purify us from all unrighteousness."[1]

Unforgiveness is quite often the heaviest and most lethal of all emotional loads. He who carries it will eventually pay its deadly price, for no one can carry it for long and live a long and fulfilling life. To forgive is a personal choice. The one who forgives is the one who receives its reward of true self-imposed freedom.

> Unforgiveness is quite often the heaviest and most lethal of all emotional loads. He who carries it will eventually pay its deadly price, for no one can carry it for long and live a long and fulfilling life.

You've been living far too long in your own prison cell. It's now time to forgive yourself, knowing that God has already forgiven you. If you've never prayed before, I suggest that you take the time to talk to your heavenly Father, God. Acknowledge your wrongdoings and ask Him for His forgiveness. Don't be intimidated by the term prayer. Prayer is like talking to God as if you would be talking to your closest friend. Just tell Him what you did and that you're sorry about it.

Although what you did may have been done to someone else and you don't have the courage to go to that person, or that person can't be reached, you can go directly to God and state that to Him and ask for forgiveness. You may never have to directly ask the person for forgiveness for what you did.

In Grief Recovery sessions, we often don't encourage the griever to directly ask for or request forgiveness. Why? It can cause even more hurts. The decision to forgive is an action verb. It's not a feeling. You decide to grant it or accept it, even when it's not asked for. Hence, you can forgive yourself. You can also forgive the offender without them necessarily asking for it in person. This is of paramount importance. At times, facing the person and asking for forgiveness can lead to further hurt. Not to mention the fact that if you're going to wait for certain personality types to apologize to you, it will never happen. They couldn't care less.

Knowing that you're sorry for your own act of wrongdoings, or granting forgiveness to someone who wronged you, can provide an even deeper sense of self-healing.

> Knowing that you are sorry for your own act of wrongdoings or granting forgiveness to someone who wronged you can provide an even deeper sense of self-healing.

THE TOUGHEST OF ALL TASKS—FORGIVE ANYONE WHO HURTS YOU

Just as others mess up, you and I mess up. Being willing to forgive others is just as important as forgiving ourselves. In fact, most of the hurts in the world today are the result of payback. You hurt me so I'll hurt you too. If I can't hurt you, I'll hurt someone close to you, or I'll find a way to make you pay for it. This is a human-nature problem that is messing up our beautiful world. It takes a force greater than ours to propel us to stop this vicious and cruel cycle.

It has left the world in a complete state of emotional war, hurt, and hatred. It leads to civil war, world war, and family feuds. Very often, even little innocent children are caught in the crossfire of parental wars. This world cannot be a safe place until we decide to make it one. One of the ways we can do so is by stopping this payback attitude.

> This world cannot be a safe place until we decide to make it one.

Your heart won't be at peace until you decide to get rid of this payback attitude. Your heart has been aching far too long because you refuse to forgive that person who dragged you down to the mud. It's now time to let go of the pain that only you are paying for. You are suffering all alone. All it takes now is for you to forgive, not for the sake of the source of your emotional pain, but for your own sake.

> Your heart will not be at peace until you decide
> to get rid of this payback attitude.

History will never forget Mahatma Gandhi, who led an entire revolution in India from British rule and the brutality of its soldiers without hurting a single soldier who had treated them so badly. When asked why he didn't encourage his people to fight back, since the Bible says an "eye for an eye, or a tooth for a tooth," Gandhi replied, "an eye for an eye only leaves the world blind."

In short, it's in your best interest to forgive. You can't afford not to forgive. You're the sole beneficiary of your act of forgiveness. Everyone else will reap its benefit because of your action. You'll be happier and so will everyone else around you. No one can act on your behalf when it comes to forgiveness. It's an action verb. Do it and you'll change your life and your world.

BE MINDFUL OF YOUR GARDEN

The issues of the heart. The issues of the mind. That's the sole purpose of this book. In this first part, I dealt with the issues of the heart. The heart is like a garden. It thrives best when watered with love. It experiences slow death when watered with anything else. When the issues of the heart are misaligned, the issues of the mind are derailed. Because of this, everything else tends to fall apart.

We can't deal with the issues of the mind until we deal with the issues of the heart. That's why sometimes you notice that when your heart is broken, your mind is confused and you tend to make a lot of mistakes in whatever you do. You're unable to focus. You're unhappy. You tend to be depressed and unfulfilled. You have frequent episodes of sadness. Your spouse, your children, your coworkers, other family and friends notice it. Some may fail to talk to you about it for fear of aggravating it. The ones who love you and care about you the most will gently and carefully address it with you. You must listen to them. They want to help you. You must also be willing to seek help. It will not go away unless you work on it.

> The heart is like a garden. It thrives best when watered with love. It experiences slow death when watered with anything else.

As I conclude this first section on the matters of the heart, I hope I've given you food for thought. The unsolved emotional issues of your heart are at the foundation of happiness. When the heart isn't happy, the issues of the mind, our intellectual and cognitive abilities, are impaired. We can't rationally fulfill our dream. It takes a great deal of our intellect to do so. Our heart and mind are in a symbiotic relationship. Until we fix our emotions, which control our actions, we cannot act on the dreams we hold dear to our hearts.

The reason why we have such unhappy, angry people in the world today is because they fail to seek help to address their emotional issues. Unhappy people make others unhappy. An unhappy spouse makes the other spouse unhappy. Unhappy parents make their children unhappy. Unhappy children make their parents unhappy. Unhappy bosses and coworkers turn the workplace into a living hell. Most of the "hellish" behaviors stem from the root cause—unresolved issues and lack of forgiveness. This is the only factor that will greatly impact your life. How will you allow these things to affect you? How can you take responsibility to ensure your own happiness? This is paramount to move you further in the game of life. When our heart is free from these emotional pains, we can move forward with a clear conscience, a clear mind, and a heart that has become so light it can cause us to soar like an eagle. After all, the birds can fly because they take things lightly. When your heart is free from all the painful memories, you too will be able to fly like a bird. So soar!

My heart is appealing to your heart because, like you, I've been hurt far too often to count. But I've noticed that the more I let go of the hurts, the more my life is fulfilled and the healthier I get. Just as I exercise daily to maintain good health, I must equally exercise my mental strength to increase my capacity to forgive and release the negative energy so that I can live a fulfilled life. With the passing of time, it gets better and better until it becomes more natural. So will it be for you!

As you're reading, you might be reflecting on yourself, your past, or those who hurt you. I assume that you're asking yourself a myriad of questions. I know I often ask myself questions for which I have no answers. You might be asking yourself the following questions:

How can I forgive and forget that person who raped me?

How can I forgive and forget the atrocities he or she caused me?

How can I forgive and forget that spouse who divorced me and how it affected me and my children in a negative way?

How can I forgive and forget how he or she robbed me and left me in a state of indebtedness or poverty?

How can I forgive and forget the lies?

My friend, I'm not here to tell you to forget. From one broken heart to another, I'm here to beg you to let go. Choosing to let go isn't the absence of the hurt but rather the presence of the will to never allow it to dominate your life and steal away your happiness.

Your heart was made to love and to receive love. Refuse to allow your past hurts to take that away. This is what my heart is trying to convey to yours. You can't effectively move on without letting go. You don't want to survive; you want to thrive. Yes, I know it's painful, especially when your hurt comes from those you once trusted. That's why Dr. Martin Luther King, Jr. once said, "In the end, we will remember not the words of our enemies, but the silence of our friends." Yes, I know you're reflecting on how silent your friends were when they could have spoken to defend you. You feel betrayed, bitter, and angry. You have reason to be, but don't let it steal away your joy. You can't change it, but you can change your attitude towards them and the situation.

Whether you're a person of faith or not, my heart wants to point out to your heart a word of wisdom so that it can be healed. These words are so deep, so revolutionary, that if they were practiced, our world would be a better place. In fact, not even the ones who profess to be Christ's followers really understand it, much less practice it. If His followers were to put this into practice, their hearts would be as pure as "gold," mine included.

> Choosing to let go isn't the absence of the hurt but rather the presence of the will to never allow it to dominate your life and steal away your happiness.

There are some important lessons we can learn regardless of our religious status. These are the core foundation of any safe community or society:

- The first is the golden rule: "So in everything, do to others what you would have them do to you"[2]
- The second is recorded in Matthew 5:38–42 and is encapsulated in 1 Peter 3:9. They all imply, "Do not render evil for evil or reviling for reviling."[3]

After reading these passages, what is your reaction? Are we not all guilty for not doing these things? This includes everyone, regardless of your belief system or religion. Everything that happens in the world today is a result of the application or the lack thereof of these texts.

If our hearts are turned into a warzone, it's because we choose to depart from their moral lessons. When we choose to apply them in our lives, personal peace and happiness begin. This world will be a better place. If this world is not, yours must be a better place.

You can't control the actions of others, but you can control your reactions to their hostility. It's not what happens to you that matters the most but rather what happens within you.

> Freedom is a state of the mind. You cannot live it until the mind experiences it.

My heart is appealing to yours to let go so that you can experience true freedom. Freedom is a state of the mind. You cannot live it until the mind experiences it. It's for your own good, not the perpetrator. If you're not a person of faith, don't let the quotations from the Bible cause you to put this book down. You're a person of high intellect; therefore, you can get words of wisdom from anyone or anything once it's of great value.

You may have turned your nose up on the words of wisdom of the Bible, or even from God Himself, because those who are at the root cause of your hurt call themselves religious or Christians. Don't allow that to block your mind towards God. There are good and bad people everywhere. Don't mix up God and religion. God is God! He's by far too big to be contained in the box of religion. Don't allow that to cause you to turn your back on God. Be sure you learn from that experience so that you don't perpetuate the hurt.

Far too often we get hurt and despise the hurt, only to turn around and hurt others. We completely forget the pain it brought on us. Instead of stopping it, we multiply it. Let it stop with you.

> Don't mix up God and religion. God is God! He's by far too big to be contained in the box of religion.

"So whatever you wish that others would do to you, do also to them"[4] If you do this, you'll experience the true meaning of the song written by Louis Armstrong, "What a Wonderful World." When you pause to listen to the words and music of that song, you can't help but to dance to it. Just dance to it until your heart is made light by the rhythmic beats of this melody. This is the beautiful world that God created you for. If it doesn't exist for you yet, you can be the architect of it now. You can change your world starting from within, causing yourself to heal from the inside out.

> This is the beautiful world that God created you for. If it doesn't exist for you yet, you can be the architect of it now.

You can create it for yourself, even in an imperfect world. You can change your world by changing your attitude to its inevitable hurts.

Finally, as I prepare to take you to the next section of this book, the issues of the mind, I want to encourage you to lighten your heart of all emotional pains by using the guides laid out in this book. Don't allow your past, present, or future hurts to steal away your joy and happiness. Deal with them as they come. Practice doing the Completion Letter to deal with your unresolved emotional issues. If needs be, use the services of a Grief Recovery specialist to help you address your unresolved emotional issues.

These words were meant to change the world one person at a time, one person times many, until the whole world is changed. May this section on the issues of the heart settle it for you. Regardless of your emotional pain, do it for yourself. Let it all go! Make room for a new you. A new beginning! You will reap its benefits. Your heart will be glad, and your life will be even merrier! Your family will be happier. You will be healthier. You will change your own world from within.

Now, let's get working on the issues of the mind. Let's move forward!

CHAPTER SUMMARY AND ACTION STEP

In chapter five we looked at the very core of freedom—forgiveness. We now know that freedom is a state of the mind.
We cannot live it until the mind experiences it. When we
study the history of colonization, we know that no country
ever gained its independence without a fight. Freedom is
never given. It's taken by the colonized country.

The same can be true for you and for me. We should never
expect our freedom to come until we fight for it. We must
claim it. Freedom is never cheap. Our ancestors fought for it.
They paid for our freedom by their own blood. If you really
want to be free, you must work hard to obtain it. We were
born free, and our hearts will never be happy until we are
emotionally free.

As we close this section, I want you to put the unresolved
issues of your heart to rest. I am desperately appealing to you
to take the necessary step and forgive yourself. Forgive your
offenders so that you cannot just survive, but thrive. Give
yourself the gift of forgiveness and you will see the difference
it will make in your life!

SECTION II:

DEALING WITH THE ISSUES OF THE MIND

STEP 6:
EVALUATING THE ISSUES
OF THE MIND

*The state of the mind is determined
by the state of the heart.*
—Emile Maxi

WITH THE EMANCIPATION OF the heart, the mind can go wild in its imagination. Healing your mind should now be your guide to greatness. It's now time to evaluate the issues of your mind.

How is the state of your mind?

Are you feeling good about yourself?

Are you feeling emotionally free?

Are you ready to take on the challenges of life?

Are you ready to dream big dreams?

The state of our mind is determined by the state of our heart. When the heart is right, the mind will also be right. It will show in our countenance. There is a Chinese proverb that goes like this: "The will is like a cart being pulled by two horses: The mind and the emotions. Both horses need to be moving in the same direction to pull the cart forward."

The heart is emotional. The mind is intellectual. The heart was made to love and for love. The mind was made to reason. The heart cannot give any reason for its ability to love. That's all it can do and must do. When it's broken, it bleeds out tears of emotions to heal itself. That's why we usually feel better after we've shed tears. But this is temporary. When the heart shares love and receives it, it's at its best. The heart loves but can never explain why it loves. The more we try to find reasons why we love, the more it doesn't make sense. Not even the mind can understand why this organ functions the way it does.

The mind, on the contrary, is intellectual. It must have a reason for anything it does. This doesn't make sense to the organ called the heart. The heart and the mind don't speak the same language. The heart speaks "emotionally," while the mind speaks "intellectually." Yet although they don't speak the same language, there is a symbiotic relationship between the two that cannot be separated. When one is emotionally ill, the other is intellectually handicapped. When the heart is emotionally healthy, the mind is intellectually emancipated, and this allows us to be more assertive, expressive, adventurous, and confident.

Therefore, it goes without saying that the state of the mind is clearly reflected in our ability to be all that we were created to be and do all we are empowered to do. This section deals with the issues of the mind. We'll address not only the issues of the mind but also give you a push start to take you through the things you always wanted to do but were unable to because the issues of the heart weren't dealt with.

> When the heart is right, the mind will also be right. It will show in our countenance.

Winston Churchill, the former Prime Minister of Great Britain, once said, "A pessimist sees the difficulty in every opportunity; an optimist sees the opportunity in every difficulty."

Have you ever taken the time to evaluate your mindset? Are you a pessimist or an optimist? Your response to this question will determine your level of success in life. If you find that you're more on the pessimistic side, you can reprogram and retrain your mind.

Our past has a way of affecting us. Depending on our personality, some can go through the worst and still find the inner strength to move on and become very successful, while some are totally crushed by the same life events. We're all different, but one thing remains extremely important in our quest to heal—our willpower and our attitude. Regardless of what you went through, or you are going through, you can pull yourself out of the rubbles of life and its difficulties. The use of a method like neuro-linguistic programming can greatly assist you in developing what it takes to move forward. It's all about changing your thoughts and behaviors to help you reach whatever goals you've set in life.

> "A pessimist sees the difficulty in every opportunity; an optimist sees the opportunity in every difficulty." WINSTON CHURCHILL

When life has been brutally hard in the past, it's often difficult for us to move forward. It leaves some emotional scars that can be hard to ignore unless we develop the mental fortitude to use them as a driving force or stepping stone to success. Quite often, the ones who have been affected the most are those who have been emotionally abused. This abuse can be so deeply rooted that it affects your ability to believe in yourself, let alone make a name for yourself. Knowing your mental state is key. Identify the issues of your mind so that you can deal with them. The reassurance is that anyone who addresses the unresolved issues of the heart finds it much easier to address the issues of the mind, which in turn will allow them to focus on their dreams and aspirations.

We know beyond the shadow of a doubt that the central processing unit, known as the CPU, of a computer is powerful. But we also know that the mind is much more powerful than a CPU. Hence, just as a computer can be programmed to perform certain tasks, you too can program your mind to achieve absolutely anything you want to achieve in life. This is without exception. Do not limit yourself. To do so, you must go beyond the pains of the past. You must find it within you. You must believe in yourself. You must believe in your God-given abilities. You must develop a positive mental attitude!

> Do not limit yourself. To do so, you must go beyond the pains of the past. You must find it within you. You must believe in yourself. You must believe in your God-given abilities. You must develop a positive mental attitude!

Yes, I know that you might be saying to yourself that you've gone through far too much. You have nothing left inside. Don't underestimate the power within you.

Yes, that includes you! You were created with everything you need to pull the courage from within, not just to heal your broken heart but also to excel in everything you want to achieve. There's only one thing you need to do now—set your mind on that which you wish to achieve and develop the right attitude to attain it.

I won't promise that the process will be easy, but if your mind can conceive it, it can achieve it.

To move forward, you need to ensure that nothing can come between you and your ability to do so. No, nothing! Not even your past. Your past is now in the past. You must now live in the brightness of your present state of mind. The things you've always wanted to do. The things you've dreamt of but thought were unattainable. You must allow your mind to guide your own world, even when it may seem impossible to others, or even to you. You mustn't weigh your present mindset and your potential on the scale of your past but rather on the scale of your potential and your desire to achieve your dreams.

The time has come for you to allow the hope of a bright future to drive you to a state of mind to be the architect of your own future. When you're liberated from the pain of your past, you can dream God-sized dreams that can only come to fruition by God's grace and glory. It will cause others to think of you as a lunatic, but that's how it is when we allow our dream to be bigger than our size. You're no longer dealing with the past, the abuses, the name-calling, the low self-esteem. You're dealing with a new mindset that is bigger than you, a mindset that will cause you to soar higher than human thoughts can reach. This is the place where you now belong. This is where God wants you to be. Claim it. It's all yours now! Act on it! You have full power and authority to act and to do. The past is behind you. The present possibilities are so bright that they are blinding. Blinding to those who can't see it, but you can—that's what matters!

> A mindset that will cause you to soar higher than human thoughts can reach. This is the place where you now belong.

Are you ready to dream God-sized dreams that may seem impossible to the human mind? These are the kind of dreamers that God likes. They know it can't happen unless God

Himself makes it happen. He has done it for others, so He will do it for you. All it takes is for you to have the tenacity to dream it, knowing that with God, all things are possible. Don't limit what God can do for you and through you. Don't fix your gaze on how big your problems are and how limited your resources are, but rather fix your gaze on how big your God is. Learn from the Wright brothers.

If we can fly in airplanes today, it's because of their God-sized dream, which was never dreamt of before. The Wright brothers didn't even have a high school education. They didn't have any great financial means. They'd never flown in an airplane before, as airplanes only existed as a concept in their mind. Up to that point, they'd only been obsessed with birds and their ability to fly, which fueled their curiosity to explore this possibility. They didn't have any pilot training—after all, it didn't exist in their world. What did they have? A dream! A dream to create an airplane. That's all it took, coupled with tenacity. They failed to fly but they refused to give up on their dream. They learned from their mistakes but never gave up. In 1892, they opened the Wright Cycle Company, which was a bicycle repair and sales shop that they used to finance their flying experiments.

On December 17, 1903, they defied gravity and were able to fly their first airplane for only twelve seconds in North Carolina. That was the beginning of greater things to come. Because of the Wright brothers' God-sized dream, today, taking a flight across the nation or the globe is a reality.

Others didn't believe in them, and they were in unchartered territory, but they believed in themselves and their God-given ability to make it come true.

Who told you that you cannot do? Who is telling you that you don't have what it takes to make the impossible, possible! Defy them all! Defy even the paralyzing thoughts in your mind. You can do it. Yes, you can! What's your dream? It needs to be bigger than your size. It needs to be a God-sized dream. That's how God likes it so that when it's done, everyone will know that it happened—because you are blessed and anointed for greatness.

Look at all modern inventions. They all came about because someone had an obsession for something and was willing to do whatever it took to work on it until it became a reality. Some had to go through lots of trial and errors. Their will, determination, and a very high level of positive attitude propelled them to achieve their dreams. You and I are the beneficiaries of their inventions. Some failed multiple times but never gave up. Some lost all they had to the point of even filing for bankruptcy, but they never gave up until they saw the fruit of their labor. They believed in the power of making the impossible, possible, and they did. Some had great human infirmities, but they didn't let that stop them. They relied on their inner strength to make the impossible, possible. If they could do it, so can you, and so will you. Embark on your journey. Dream big. Dream God-sized dreams. If there's no path, create one. Go and make history!

CHAPTER SUMMARY AND ACTION STEP

What is the state of your mind? In this chapter, we looked at the issue of the mind, and now it's time for you to pass into action. Don't pity yourself, and allow no one to pity you. There is greatness in you. You must reach out to it, as it won't come out unless you dig deep. Your past hardship must not define your success. You've gone through a bad separation or divorce and have been disappointed. Don't let that stop you. Find your inner strength and pull yourself up from under the feeling of despair and discouragement. You've lost your job and can't seem to get the one you really desire. Don't let that stop you. It may be time for you to start your own company and become the one to hire others.

You may be in an abusive relationship and don't know how to get out due to your financial distress. You don't have to stay and endure the abuse. Don't settle for less than what you're worth. You may be struck with a health issue that leaves you bewildered; it's not a death sentence. You can change that. Do what it takes to address it. Dream big. Dream God-sized dreams! For emphasis, let me repeat the questions you need to answer to evaluate and to address your own issues:

How is the state of your mind now?

Are you feeling better about yourself?

Are you feeling emotionally free?

Are you ready to take the next challenge in your life?

Are you ready to dream big dreams?

Are your ready to take the next step in your life?

What are your big dreams?

Are you going to work hard and smart to turn your big dreams into a reality?

God can help me
→ see the future

→ Forgive the past.

→ God, help me to be willing to serve - whatever needs to be done,

STEP 7:
POSITIONING YOURSELF
FOR SUCCESS

Life is a journey. Its detours can be eventful,
but our attitude will make the difference.
—Emile Maxi

YOUR JOURNEY TO JOY and happiness begins now. Are you ready? One of the most thrilling inventions of modern time is the Global Positioning System, commonly known as the GPS. The website www.aerospace.org gives a detailed history of the GPS. It has made life easier in a time when the world has become a global village. Everything is now at our fingertips.

In 2003, my wife, June, and I packed our car and took our two girls, Juneile and Nicole, who were about four and eight years old at the time, from Montreal, Canada on a three-day drive to Disney World in Orlando, Florida. We were going there for the first time and didn't know the way. How did we get there?

In those days, GPS devises weren't very common. If you could get one, it would cost an arm and a leg. The most common thing to do was to go to MapQuest and download a printed version. This was our guide. MapQuest was our faithful companion. It took us to our destination safe and sound, but it was very eventful, to say the least.

Traveling with two girls under ten years of age, every so often they'd ask, "Mommy, Daddy, are we there yet?" When I think back on all the detours we encountered, the traffic jams when we reached a busy city in the middle of rush hour, and the number of times we got lost, I realize that had we not made up our minds to enjoy the journey, our trip would have been a disaster. Life is a journey; its detours can be eventful, but our attitude will make the difference.

Today we can purchase a GPS at a reasonable cost, often for less than 300 dollars, and off we go. Nowadays, you don't even have to buy one because most Smartphones give you access to a GPS right in the palm of your hands, or on the dashboard of your vehicle. This makes taking a trip to a new place easy. We can plan our vacation and head to that destination with few worries.

The real issue I've observed is that we plan our vacations far better than we plan our lives. Some want to succeed in life but fail to put in the work to maximize their success.

How can you position yourself for success? Since the beginning of this book, we've been talking about being emotionally healthy. If we don't address the issues in our lives, they will affect us and be a stumbling block in our path to success.

If you know that you're stuck in the rut of life more than anyone can fathom, never lose sight of the fact that you're unstoppable. Don't be so focused on the destination that you can't enjoy the detours. This will make a huge difference in your life. Sometimes the detours can be as important as the destination.

I don't know the state of your mind, but I want you to stay with me. Why? Just like you, I've been battered, bruised, and shaken by life's crucibles, so I know how it can feel. I've known a lot of people who are successful today who went through life's grindery. You are not alone. I can identify with you.

To move forward in life, you need to position yourself for success. It all begins in the mind and placing yourself in the right environment. Let me suggest that regardless of how good or bad the past has been for you, if you've never made it, you can make it. If you've made it but lost it, you can make it again. You can use the past to inspire you to success, and you define success. You are never too wealthy that you can't go penniless, and you're never too penniless that you can't be wealthy.

> Remember this, you are never too wealthy that you cannot go penniless, or you are never too penniless that you cannot be wealthy.

We began this journey by taking care of the issues of the heart, the unresolved emotional issues. I hope that with the passing of time and by doing the exercises, you'll be in a better place to move to this new aspect, the life coach. In chapters six through ten we'll deal with the issues of the mind. To do this, we'll use our internal GPS to guide us forward on our journey. It's of utmost importance that the process is interesting, rewarding, and fun.

Let's assume you're right in front of me either via Zoom, on the phone, or in person for a ten-week journey of life coaching, and this is the first session. Where would you want us to begin? Please bear in mind that as a life coach I don't coach the person's problem but the person.

Knowing why you need a coach is as important as what you want to achieve in the coaching sessions. I hope to be of great assistance to you as you move forward in your quest to achieve your goals in life.

Life coaching is a relatively new field that emerged from the field of psychology about thirty years ago. Its aim is to inspire individuals to be what they always wanted to be. It took its roots from what some refer to as positive psychology. In life coaching, we work with adults of any age in any area of their life to help them unlock their full potential. We don't deal with mental illness, though, so if an individual has mental issues, they need to seek help from a mental health professional.

WHY USE THE SERVICES OF A LIFE COACH?

Most successful people started their journey with a life coach, and most of them still have a life coach in their lives. To be effective, this initially needs to be a commitment of at least eight weeks, once a week for about an hour. Thereafter, you can follow up with your life coach on a consultation basis, depending on what you want to achieve and the size of your project.

Often people have lots of dreams and aspirations, but unfortunately, they're stuck in the "thinking" stage. Ten years ago they had great dreams, plans, and aspirations. Ten years later, they're still dreaming. That's why I said earlier that some of us plan our vacations better than we plan our lives. Having a life coach with whom you share your dream will help to turn your dream into a reality.

Think of the coach of your favorite sports team. When the team loses too many games, what often takes place? They fire the coach. Why? Because the role of the coach is to train and empower the team to play to the best of their ability. The coach doesn't play the game, but he or she observes, guides, is proactive, knows the strength and the weaknesses of each team member, motivates, inspires, trains the team to use the right techniques, puts the team through the right training, and pulls out what the team didn't even know they had within. Coupled with the right attitude, they do their best to win the game.

Most of the time we're not successful in life because of the absence of a coach. We have dreams and aspirations, but we fail to act on them because of a lack of motivation and/or a structure to help us accomplish them. Quite often, this role is played by a mother, a father, a relative, or a trusted friend. We need them in our lives. If you don't have one, you need one. You too can be a coach to someone else. In fact, the best way to discover your dream is to help someone accomplish theirs.

> The best way to discover your dream is to help someone accomplish theirs.

You know how long you've been dreaming about achieving that goal you cherish; it's time for you to invest in yourself. Any amount of money spent on yourself is not an expense but an investment.

Maybe you're not where you would have liked to be just because you neglected that aspect of your life. Don't be penny-wise and pound-foolish. If you fail to invest in yourself, no one else will. The fact that you purchased this book is a clear indication that you're investing in yourself. Stay on! My objective is to move you to action, one step at a time.

I want to inspire you by looking at your dream, turning your dream into your vision, your vision into your mission, your mission into an action plan, and your action plan into your success.

> I want to inspire you by looking at your dream, turning your dream into your vision, your vision into your mission, your mission into an action plan, and your action plan into your success.

DO NOT NEGLECT YOUR CURRENT POSITION

Some undermine where they are in their current journey, and some fail to start because they argue that it's not the right position. They might be too messed up. They may have too much baggage. They may feel that they don't have what it takes. They find all the excuses to avoid starting on their road to success.

Your journey to success has only one location—your starting point. It's unique to you. This means that wherever you are currently positioned is where you must start from. Don't be ashamed. Make the best of it. There's a reason why the windshield is much wider than the rearview mirror. The windshield is to give you a broader view of where you're going. Focus on what's ahead. The rearview mirror is there only to remind you of where you're coming from; you aren't heading back.

If you've used a GPS lately, you'll understand that although you haven't necessarily entered your current location, its internal intelligence recognizes its current location. If the GPS doesn't recognize its current location, it's difficult or impossible to know the different possible routes available to take you to your destination.

Similarly, to go anywhere, you ought to know where you are now. That's your starting point. It may not be your best position, but it's your position and that's the reality. Your journey to success begins right there.

Unfortunately, that "current location" may be a painful relationship that has destroyed your self-worth. It may be a tough financial problem. It may be some other forms of abuse. It may be a health-related issue. May I remind you that this is only temporary. You are about to depart from it. You're only stuck there for a while, but things are going to get better the moment you know where you need to be and where you will be in the future. It gives hope, and hope will keep you alive. Never let it die. Hope is all that we have. If it dies, we might as well die too.

When you get to where you really want to be, you'll be proud of yourself when you look back. You'll be stronger, not just for yourself but also for those who would have been stuck in the rut of life and need your help. It takes one who was in it to help one who is in it. Let that one be you!

> It takes one who was in it to help one who is in it. Let that one be you!

ELIMINATING NEGATIVE INFLUENCES

As part of positioning yourself for success, one of the things I would suggest is that you get rid of negative things that may hold you back. This could be one or all of the following:

- negative thoughts

- procrastination
- bad company
- addiction
- pessimistic influences
- emotional baggage

You can't afford to embark on this journey and still carry the heavy-weight emotional stuff. They weren't meant to be taken on this journey. They have no place in your life. You can't move forward with them; they will hinder you. You must lay them aside, otherwise they'll keep you back.

You must be intentional in this journey. In the journey of life, there are many unwanted and unplanned detours, but that's part of the journey. We have no choice over that. However, we must remain focused and positive. There's no time to gaze over our shoulders. We must maintain absolute focus and self-control, even when we feel we've lost control.

If you feel that your internal GPS, and by this I mean your mind, isn't giving you a clear sense of direction, then read great books, listen to webinars and great speeches that will motivate you. Have inspiring people in your life. I hope it will inspire you to action.

As we prepare to bring this chapter to a close, let me ask you a very important question: What do you need to do to position yourself for success?

Your road to success begins with where you are now. It may not be the best or ideal, but it's where you are and that's all you have. Use it to your advantage and don't complain, as it won't help you. Be positive. Be proactive. Be intentional. Your attitude will make all the difference. If you don't have a positive and winning attitude, no one can help you. Before you can deal with your external world, you may have to look in the mirror. The person you see in the mirror is the person you need to start working on. Yes, that's you!

All the past hurts may have shattered you, but they didn't break you—unless you allow them to. Though difficult and harsh, use them to be that resilient person you ought to be.

Let nothing stop you from achieving your goals. Be positive! Be resilient! Position yourself for success by making yourself a victor, not a victim of your circumstances, though heart-breaking and paralyzing. You will make it! The power lies in you. Reach out for it.

CHAPTER SUMMARY AND ACTION STEP

We all live under the same sky, but we don't all share or see the same horizon. Why? Because we see it from different perspectives. We all don't have the same attitude. Positioning yourself for success is a choice. It requires self-discipline and determination. It requires you to not make yourself a victim of the past, or of your circumstances. It requires you to adopt a positive mental attitude. These are the only weapons you have against life's warfare. Use them and you will be unstoppable.

The journey will never be exactly how you would have liked it. It will be filled with unexpected plans and unwanted detours. You have no choice then. Accept them as part of the journey and make use of everything life throws at you. Use them as stepping stones towards greater things. You will be wiser and better.

- Are you being inspired?
- Are you positioning yourself for success?
- Are you prepared to leave behind the things that are hindering you to reach your God-sized dream and potential?
- Are you prepared to take that leap of faith to reach your maximum potential?
- What's stopping you?

Let's go! Let's take it to the next step. Let's dream the big dreams!

STEP 8:
ALLOWING YOUR
DREAM TO BE THE WIND
BENEATH YOUR WINGS

When God created you, He set no limit over you.
Make the sky the standard of your growth potential.
—Emile Maxi

CAN YOU RECALL THE God-sized dreams you had when you were growing up? What stopped you from achieving them? Have you ever thought of taking a leap of faith that was destined to fail unless God Himself intervened?

God seems to be very interested in these types of dreams. When our dreams are much bigger than our size and we know they can't come to fruition except by the intervention of the Almighty Himself, He steps in. In such a case, we can't take the credit for fulfilling the God-sized dreams. They are far too big for any human being to accomplish.

If you could only recall the many miracles He's performed in your life, you wouldn't allow anything to come between your shallow dreams and your God-sized dreams. He wants you to think the impossible because He is the God of the impossible. Impossible things can only be accomplished by the God of the impossible. So stop your shallow thinking! Put Him to the test!

> If you could only recall the many miracles He's performed in your life, you wouldn't allow anything to come between your shallow dreams and your God-sized dreams.

Far too long you've been hoping for something great to happen to you but you haven't taken the step of faith. Hope is great, but it's time to put your dream to the acid test.

Quite often, our dreams are shaped by our environment. We may have great dreams for our lives, but circumstances of life impact them based on our past or present experiences. For someone in an abusive relationship or coming out of one, all the great dreams and aspirations for a loving and lasting relationship come to a halt as the result of the fear of stepping into another abusive relationship.

For a girl who's been sexually abused by her father, the damaging effect of that abuse may pose a potential problem to future romantic relationships if she doesn't seek professional help.

A boy who witnessed his father mistreat his mother may not have learned the important human social and romantic skills to be able to treat his wife with love, respect, and admiration. In fact, he may even lack the social skills to treat any woman with respect.

A boy who didn't grow up with a real father figure at home may not know how to treat his family because he has no point of reference. He may not even have the right skills to be either a great father or a great husband unless he acknowledges the issue and seeks to emulate some great men in his life. The greater problem is inability to see God as our heavenly Father when our earthly fathers fail us so miserably. It can be hard to reconcile the two.

Someone who grew up in poverty may have great dreams and aspirations but fail to take the leap of faith just because they don't want to jeopardize the little that they now have. They may give up on their dreams entirely for fear of failing. I've worked with a lot of people who had great dreams, but with the passing of time, they allowed themselves to stop dreaming because they couldn't deal with the improbabilities of life. I've noticed one thing about these people. Their true date of death is not the date registered on their death certificate. The process of gradual death for them starts the day they stop dreaming. Conversely, some people start living the day they start dreaming.

- What's your dream?

- If you don't have a dream, associate yourself with people who have great dreams, and you'll end up developing one by association.
- Read great books that can inspire you.
- Listen to great speeches that will move you.

You had great dreams, but your hard life took them all away from you. You're barely surviving. You can't dream because there's nothing to dream about. You've failed and been let down so many times. A voice within constantly keeps reminding you of the things you heard in the past, so you're afraid to even try. Prove that voice wrong! Dream on! Let your heart come alive by the drive of your dreams.

CHASING AFTER YOUR DREAM

When we were younger, our parents had great dreams for us. At times, we even follow their dreams to please them. When we get into adulthood, we follow the trend and choose a career path that will guarantee us a paycheck, only to find later that we don't like it. Since we have no other options, we stick to it just for the salary, although it brings no real and lasting happiness. To strike a balance, we keep our day job so that we can pay the bills, but we try to have a side job, hoping that it's what we always wanted to do. So we test the waters before setting both feet in fully, hoping that it will bring us that sense of satisfaction and self-actualization. The cycle continues until we hit it. Quite often, we're restless until we finally fulfill our personal dream. For some, unfortunately, they never find it.

If you're not living out your dream now, it's not because it's lost but because it's suppressed. Your dream is never lost! It just needs to be rekindled. That's the passion within. No one can extinguish it but you. Your circumstances may affect it. Your past may dampen it, but it is always very much alive in your heart and mind. When there are many unresolved issues in the heart, it creates a sense of a loss of identity, low self-esteem, and bewilderment. Hence, we are just surviving. You were made not just to survive but to thrive.

> Your dream is never lost! It needs to be rekindled. That's the passion within. No one can extinguish it but you. Your circumstances may affect it. Your past may dampen it, but it is always very much alive. Where? In your heart and mind.

When the issues of the heart are resolved, we can dream again. Our dreams always remain in the treasure box of our heart. This section will take you through the process of turning your dreams into reality.

You need to chase after your dreams and reflect on them. You need to let them put a smile on your face again. Make them the reason for your existence. They're not dead. They're resting in the comfort of your heart and mind, waiting for the right opportunity to arise. Now is the time. Are you ready? Go! Awake them!

It's said that the two most important dates in the life of a person are:

- The day they were born.
- The day they discover why they were born.

Let me get you to think:

- When were you born?
- When did you discover why you were born?

I'm trying to help you think of the day you discovered your passion, your dream. What are your dreams? Are you currently living out that dream? Don't be timid. It's been a long time since you revisited the dreams of your life:

- The dreams of your teenage years.
- The dream of your romantic life.
- The dream of your professional career.
- The dream of achieving your desired weight.
- The dream of regaining control over your health.
- The dream of being financially independent.
- Any other dreams that are important to you.

List your dreams so that you can look at them. They may not be real yet, but in your mind, they are. Someone else may not be able to see them, but you can. That's the most important thing. Your dream must matter to you first before they can matter to someone else. Others will believe in them only if you're bold enough to believe in your own dream.

THE POWER OF A DREAM

Never underestimate the power of your dream. Regardless of how far down you are in a rut, your dream should be the wind beneath your wings. Never let go of it. That's what will pull you out of the rut. Think of this true story.

Monty Roberts was a high school student. His teacher gave an assignment in which the students had to write an essay about their future dream. In his essay, he wrote that his dream was to own a 200-acre ranch and raise thoroughbred racehorses. Unfortunately, his teacher never believed that was possible because he was living in a camper in the back of pickup truck, hence she gave him an F. However, his teacher was kind enough to give him an opportunity to redeem himself by rewriting his essay so that he could get a higher grade. Monty Roberts believed so much in his dream that he said to his teacher, "you can keep your F. I'm keeping my dream."[1]

After leaving high school, he worked hard at what mattered most to him. Eventually, Monty's dream came true. He's now the proud owner of a 154-acre ranch in Solvang, California, which is home to world-class thoroughbred racehorses. You can read more about Monty Roberts' stories at: https://montyroberts.com.

Let no one tell you that your dream is too big. In fact, when you read about the history of inventions, they all came to fruition because the dreamers believed in their dreams even when they were ridiculed and opposed.

Think of this. On May 25, 1961, the President of the United States of America, John F. Kennedy, stood before congress and proposed that the USA should commit itself to achieving a goal that was very daring: within a decade, landing a man on the moon and returning him safely to the Earth.

The fact that it had never been done before didn't mean it couldn't be done. Of course, not everyone was impressed with the idea. A Gallup poll indicated that 58% of Americans were in opposition. But because President JFK and others believed it, on July 20, 1969, the National Aeronautics and Space Administration (NASA) achieved this daring goal within the decade specified. That day, at 10:56 p.m. ET, the American astronaut Neil Armstrong set his left foot on the lunar surface and famously declared: "That's one small step for man, one giant step for mankind."[2]

I was about three years old at that time, and my little mind didn't really understand all it entailed, but I did notice it had everyone's attention. It all happened because of a man's dream.

You can learn more about it by visiting: https://www.jfkli-brary.org/node/16986.

BEWARE OF THE DREAM-KILLERS

You have dreams and you'll have many more. Beware of who you share your dreams with. Some will kill your dreams from conception. You may have lots of great friends, but not all of them can handle the expansion of your mind. This doesn't mean that they're bad people. It simply means that they all have a particular role in your life. The expansion of your dream may not be their forte.

> You may have lots of great friends, but not all of them can handle the expansion of your mind.

They may have other roles in your life, but not to help nurture your dreams into maturity. For President JFK's dream to come true, he had to have the right people at the table. For your dream to come into maturity, you too need to have the right people at your table.

AVOID HAVING TOO MANY DREAMS AT THE SAME TIME

What's your dream? To have too many dreams and expecting to do them all at once can be so daunting that it becomes discouraging. I have a friend who is very talented, well-educated, and brilliant. I've known him for a long time. He has lots of ideas and dreams. They're great dreams, but unfortunately, after over 25 years of listening to him talk about his dreams and not even one coming to fruition, I noticed that he grew cold and at times cast blame as to why his dreams were not fulfilled.

If you're going to succeed in life, it's never a good idea to cast blame, as it helps no one. You should always be willing to take full responsibility for your actions. No one can stop you. Not even your circumstances can stop you. The only person who can stop you is you!

Don't get to into the same habit as my friend. Ensure that you're not only dreaming but that you're putting your dream to the acid test. I suggest that you follow the steps below:

1. IDENTIFY YOUR DREAMS

I've been working with people from all walks of life with lots of dreams and aspirations. At times some of them have so many dreams that they can't easily identify a specific one that they need to accomplish. Quite often, this bring lots of frustration and, at times, even a sense of failure. Very often they even cast blame on their partner, their spouse, their parents, their education, their environment, or the government.

Sometimes they even attribute their failure to God, stating if He wanted, He would give them a sense of clarity. I don't buy any of that. I don't believe that God created robots. He created us with all the faculties and the abilities to be and do whatever we want.

God has already blessed us with everything we need to succeed, so we must utilize His many gifts to our advantage. I don't believe in casting blame. It's important that we take full responsibility for our success and failure.

In a recent online seminar I attended, John C. Maxwell said, "When things do not work the way we had hoped, we must be prepared to:

- learn
- unlearn
- adjust
- relaunch

This is so true. We can't keep doing the same thing repeatedly and expect different results. We can't allow ourselves to be stuck in our routines, even when they're not working for us. Life isn't easy. Nothing will happen until we make it happen. In the process of making things happen, we must always bear in mind that failure is a part of the process. Failure is part of learning!

As your life coach through the printed pages of this book, I suggest that you make use of a notebook. Consider this notebook as your "Dream Book." Start with the first page. You'll need to keep this book close and dear to you. Years from now, it will remind you of where you started so that you can celebrate your achievements or accomplishments.

This can be used for short-term and long-term dreams. You can determine what short-term or long-term mean to you. For some, short-term may mean one month to two years. Long-term may mean three to five years. You determine yours based on your age and the urgency of your dream and plans.

Start with page 1. At the top of the page, write: "My Dream Ideas." Draw a line in the middle of the page so that you end up with two columns. In column 1, write: "My Dreams." In column 2, write: "My Top Dream"

In column 1, write down everything you've dreamt of. As you write them down, assign a number to each (1, 2, 3, etc.). In this case, it's okay to list all your dreams. Over the period of your life, there are many things you'll want to accomplish. You need to be able to see them so that you don't lose sight of them. But you do need to avoid doing too many at the same time, so the following steps are of paramount importance. Now, let's work on the second step—prioritizing your dreams in order of importance.

2. PRIORITIZE YOUR MOST IMPORTANT DREAMS IN ORDER OF IMPORTANCE

This section will help you avoid being overwhelmed by your myriad of dreams and getting stuck. From column 1, pick your number 1 dream that you're passionate about and want to achieve first. Put it in column 2. This now becomes your most important dream that you will commit to work on first until it's accomplished.

3. SETTING A DATE FOR YOUR DREAM TO BE FULFILLED

It's wise to state when you want to accomplish or fulfill this dream. This will ensure that you're not illusive and nonchalant.

Transfer the other dreams in column 1 to column 2 in order of importance. As you look at them in column 1, you'll have more clarity in terms of what's more important to you. Assign a date when you want to see them accomplished. Keep checking your progress and avoid procrastination. Provide encouragement and celebrate small wins.

4. WHY DO YOU WANT TO PURSUE THIS DREAM?

As you get to this part, it's very important to know why you want to pursue this dream. Enter your "why" in your Dream Journal. This will be the wind beneath your wings to carry you to your ultimate destination. When you have a sense of purpose, knowing "why you do what you do," it will drive your passion. Any obstacles you meet along the way will be met with strong resistance because your sense of determination will be greater than the obstacles. You won't accept a NO for an answer. A great way to fuel your passion is to listen to others who had great dreams and were willing to put their lives at stake to accomplish them. In fact, their passion for their dream became so strong that they knew that even if they were to die in the process, their dream would live on and be fulfilled by others.

When you can clearly define the "why" of your dream and have others espouse your dream, you will quickly discover that your greatest legacy won't be just your dream, but future generations will be inspired by your dream and will gladly take it to higher heights.

Let me use myself to help clarify this for you. I've been involved in counseling of all sorts for thirty years. I've seen a lot of emotional pain and suffering over the years, and I've educated myself in different fields so that I can be of greater help to those who are going through emotional pain and suffering so, I became a Grief Recovery specialist and life coach. But I noticed that I don't have enough time to help as many people as I would have liked. Therefore, I decided to write this book on emotional health. Why?

- I want to help as many hurting people as possible in the shortest possible time in the comfort of their homes
- I want to help those "emotionally hurting people" get unstuck because part of unresolved emotional issues is the inability to move forward. Hence, I wrote this

book, which deals with the issues of the heart and the mind. By this, I make it easier, cheaper, and accessible and doable to them.

- I want to inspire these "emotionally hurting people" to do the things that inspire them.

Do you see how the "Why I Want to Pursue My Dream" as a writer becomes meaningful? It now becomes meaningful to you and to me. But I couldn't do it alone. A long list of people made the publishing of this book a reality. Similarly, you mustn't be egocentric about your dream. It's not about you. It's about why you do what you do. For me, it's to help people! If you're reading this book, you're one of them!

Take Dr. Martin Luther King Jr., for instance. When you listen to his speech, "I Have a Dream,"[3] you'll notice that he doesn't only move others to dream with him, but he fuels them to action. It all happened at a time when he and others believed that the political and social landscape of the United States of America needed to change. They had to peacefully fight against racial discrimination and social injustice.

Dr. Martin Luther King Jr. lost his life defending this cause, and he never saw its fulfillment in its glory. But others dreamt with him and continue to fight against racial discrimination and social injustice today. Why? He knew the why, and so did his supporters. Your dream must be bigger than you.

To inspire you, I would like to encourage you to find at your local library or online the full speech of Dr. Martin

Luther King Jr. entitled: "I have a dream." I like to listen to great speeches. They inspire and move me, so I'd like it to inspire and move you too. It was delivered on August 28, 1963, on the steps of the Lincoln Memorial. Dr. Martin Luther King Jr. died a long time now but his speech lives on.

I am a student of history, so I love to read and listen to great speeches. They give me a sense of passion to do the things I like to do but lack the courage.

When you read Dr. Martin Luther King Jr.'s speech and understand how it moved not just Black people but also Caucasians and other ethnic groups, you get a glimpse as to why they shared in the dream and sacrificed their lives to bring about change in the United States of America.

We all have dreams, but we can't fulfill our dreams alone. We need others with like passion to help turn them into reality. Your dream needs to be bigger than your size so that you can grow into it. When you share it with the right people, they'll help you achieve the unfathomable. So let's look at the next step.

> Your dream needs to be bigger than your size so that you can grow into it. When you share it with the right people, they'll help you achieve the unfathomable.

5. SHARE YOUR DREAM WITH THE RIGHT PEOPLE

Like Dr. Martin Luther King, Jr., you can get the right people to share your dream and have them on your team. Whatever your dream may be, big or small, you can make it happen. Don't allow fear to cripple you. Believe it is possible even when you don't have all the ducks in a row.

The fact that the dream was conceived in your mind doesn't mean that you must be the sole person to nurture it and bring it to maturity. Lots of people would like to be part of something big. The fact that someone is close to you doesn't mean that they'll share your dream. You must know them well enough to trust them with your dream. As you share your dream with others, even those you believe might support you, be prepared to be ridiculed. If you are, don't take it personally. They just aren't at your level yet.

You must muster the courage and the resilience to continue to move forward until you find the right match. Nothing comes easily in life. You must be prepared to pay the price and work hard to fulfill your dream, but never at the expense of your health or your family life. Regardless of how important your dream is to you, your health and your family come first. Take time to smell the roses. Take time to enjoy quality time with your family.

As a pastor, I spend a lot of time with people who are sick and, at times, at the end of their life. When reflecting on their lives, none of them ever said that they wished they'd spent more time at the office or in their business. Their last words before taking their last breath is always: "Pastor, I wish I'd spent more time with my family."

Don't make that mistake! Don't sacrifice your family life on the altar of your dream. Don't sacrifice your health either. You must dream because it will breathe life in you and to you, but it must not take your life in the process. While dreaming and fulfilling your dream, you must make it fun and rewarding.

> Don't sacrifice your family life on the altar of your dream. Don't sacrifice your health either. You must dream because it will breathe life in you and to you, but it must not take your life in the process.

As you share your dream with the right people, always keep an open mind. They will add a lot of value to the fulfillment of your dream. Their role is not only to listen to you but also to be a catalyst, a funnel through which your dream can become even bigger.

Don't use them, work with them. Don't manipulate them, empower them. If they're going to help make your dream bigger than it was conceived, they need to be valued. Some of them will be even more talented than you are and gifted in their area of expertise. Listen to them; let them have their fingerprints on your dream. They'll add great value to you and your dream. This leads us to the next step—know your strengths and your weaknesses.

6. KNOW YOUR STRENGTHS AND YOUR WEAKNESSES

God knows why He didn't give us strengths only. There is a reason. It keeps us humble and interdependent. We depend on others to complement our areas of weaknesses, so don't be ashamed to say you don't know and to seek help from people who have more knowledge, experience, and expertise than you. Failing to do this will slow your progress. In fact, it might even cripple your dream. As the proverb goes: "No one is an island; no one stands alone." It takes strength to stand alone, but it takes wisdom to seek help and to lean on others.

> It takes strength to stand alone, but it takes wisdom to seek help and to lean on others.

Knowing your limitations in relation to your dream and the areas of giftedness of your key players is the key to your success.

If you need to pay key people to help you reach your objectives, be willing to remunerate them well. Depending on what you want to achieve, paying people might get you there much faster.

If you're going to use volunteers, be sure of their total commitment, expertise, and work ethic. You don't want to stall your progress. Regardless, whether remunerated or volunteering, they're adding great value to your dream. Add great value to them. There's a proverb that says: "What is appreciated, appreciates."

Your supporters will have people in their own circle who come on board by association. They'll help you in more ways than one. Love them. Treat them kindly. Invest in them. Equip them. Respect them. Be honest with them. Value them. Be very generous in showing appreciation. Help them to achieve their own dreams. They will be loyal to you for life and will help take you to heights you never dreamed of reaching. Go! Let your dream be the wind beneath your wings.

CHAPTER SUMMARY AND ACTION STEP

Are you enjoying life to the fullest? If the answer to this question is no, then you need to find your passion. I suggest that you go back as far as you can and try to locate that date and time you were passionate about something. When you find it, spend some time thinking about its positive effects on you. Did it bring a smile on your face? Did it make your heart pound in excitement?

This is what you need! Life is too short to live without meaningful excitement. Whatever that might be to you, go for it. You don't want to reach at the end of your life with only regrets for the things you really wanted to do in life but never got around to. You were created to enjoy life to the fullest. Never forget this fact: The two most important days in someone's life are:

- The day they were born
- The day they discovered why they were born

If you haven't yet discovered your "why," it's time to explore it.

I believe that we all have a dream. In fact, lots of them! Circumstances of life may suppress them, but they're very much alive and lying dormant in the treasurer box of our heart. Go! Wake them up! Rekindle them! Life will re-enter your body!

God created you to have big dreams. God-sized dreams. What's your dream?

STEP 9:
PASSING INTO ACTION

A dream without action is only a fantasy.
—Emile Maxi

WE DON'T LACK DREAMS. We lack action. By this I mean we lack acting on our dreams. I've talked with a lot of people who have lots of dreams and aspirations, but they remain in a state of constant dreams. They move from one dream to the next but never focus on "the one dream" and work on it until it becomes a reality.

If you have dreams, believe in them. Why don't you put them to the acid test? What are you afraid of? You won't know if it will work until you pass into action. Even if you fail, at least you've learned. If you're afraid to lose, you'll never win. No one has succeeded in anything in life who didn't first experience failure. Quite often, our fortune lies in our misfortune. Wanting to play it safe is one of the things that keeps back a lot of dreams. Don't underestimate your misfortune, for in it lies your fortune.

> Don't underestimate your misfortune,
> for in it lies your fortune.

All great inventions and achievements began with a dream, and they all came to fruition because the "dreamers" had the internal fortitude and enough wisdom to take the necessary steps to turn them into reality. To do so takes great courage. Based on my experience, people with a rough past due to unresolved emotional issues are so battered emotionally that their self-esteem is low and they lose confidence in themselves, making them unable to achieve anything. Often they're caught in a circle of verbal and/or physical abuse. Their judgment is impaired, so they keep repeating the same mistakes as they try to mend their broken hearts. For some reason, they tend to attract the losers who drag them down further into the pit of misery and unhappiness.

For some, these misfortunes may affect their dreams and aspirations, while for others, they might give them more impetus to work harder to move themselves forward. If for any reason you find that you drifted a bit from your aspirations, make no mistake—your childhood dreams are still very much alive, but your circumstances may cause you to feel stuck. To move on, you must address your environmental issue.

LOOKING AT YOUR ENVIRONMENT
AND YOUR MINDSET

While your future success isn't determined by your environment, it does greatly contribute to it. Most people who migrated to the USA or Canada will tell you that they decided to migrate because of the opportunities they lacked in their country of origin. Similarly, if you have big dreams but the environment in which you're living doesn't encourage you, your ability to succeed will be impacted. This doesn't mean you can't succeed anywhere, but you will have to work against the odds. Therefore, you'll have to work twice as hard to accomplish your dream. Even in these rich countries, some people struggle to make ends meet. What's the problem?

Some of the poorest nations on earth have some of the richest people, while some of the richest nations have some of the poorest people. Why? I want to believe that either of the two is a state of mind. It doesn't matter where you live—you can make it. You don't have to change your country to succeed. All you need to change is your mindset. Most of the time, this is what prevents us from fulfilling our dreams and aspirations. Change your mindset, change your world. When you have the right mindset, it will direct you to where you need to be, who you need to surround yourself with, and what you need to do to get your desired outcome.

> It doesn't what matter where you live—you can make it. You don't have to change your country to succeed. All you need to change is your mindset.

The First World or industrialized countries are leading the way in innovation and almost all aspects of life because they attract some of the best minds from other countries, giving them great opportunities to achieve their dreams and aspirations. They end up making significant contributions to these industrialized countries. The immigration policies of the USA, Canada, and other industrialized countries are based on attracting people based on their education and achievements in their homeland. Therefore, if you have dreams and aspirations and are willing to work hard, you can make it.

You can make it anywhere regardless of where you are, although the environmental and political systems of some countries make it easier to succeed.

If you're going to put your dream to the acid test and be successful, you may want to address these key questions:

- What do you want to achieve?
- Why you want to achieve it?
- Who can help you achieve it?
- How will they help you achieve it?
- How will they benefit from it?
- What are the other variables to consider to mitigate risks, setbacks, opportunities, obstacles, and options?

Let's address each area as mentioned above.

DETERMINE WHAT YOU WANT TO ACHIEVE

What is your purpose in life? Take a moment at the end of this chapter to reflect on this very important question.

Finding your purpose will help change your life. For some people, it will be something as simple as the calling that Mother Teresa felt—caring for the less fortunate. This gave her the greatest satisfaction. When a group of American missionaries visited her and witnessed how she was selflessly caring for the orphans, they exclaimed that they wouldn't do it for a million dollars, to which she replied, "Neither would I." Mother Teresa wasn't known to be wealthy, but her sense of purpose in life gave her the joy that few millionaires possess.

Determining your dream and what you want to achieve is very important. To find your purpose, you'll need to look internally and see what tickles your sense of happiness. What makes you smile? What brings you the greatest sense of satisfaction? How does it change the lives of others? Trust me, when you see it, you'll know it. Your heart will leap for joy. You won't have to earn a dollar to be happy, but if you can use that sense of purpose to bring you an income, it will be even better. You'll work tirelessly on it, and you won't feel the stress of it.

Someone once said, "A career is what you are paid for. A calling is what you are made for." Wow! That's so powerful. If you have a career that only gives you a paycheck, but you don't have that calling for which you were made, it can rob you of a sense of purpose, and you might end up being a miserable person.

However, if you can combine both the career and the calling, no one can stop your progress. Better yet, if you can turn your calling into an income-generating adventure, not only will you be the happiest, but the person who receives your service will also be happier. Why? You will serve with a sense of joy, contentment, and fulfillment. It's a win-win for all.

The quality of your service will be at its peak. You'll serve with a smile. A smile is contagious. A smile begets a smile, and your own world will experience that change. We know that for a fact. When we're not happy at what we do, we tend to be frowny, grumpy, and unpleasant. We tend to count the hours and can't wait to clock out.

You may be poor in cash, but you're rich in ideas and dreams, so turn them into action and spring back into total financial independence. Don't allow the verbal and sexual abuses to keep you in a state of fear, hate, and depression. Leap to your feet, take control of your life, and thrive. Yes, you can make it!

If you're down, it will take someone standing on higher ground to pull you out. There are a host of people waiting and willing to pull you up. Through the pages of this book, I'm here to do just that for you. So find your team. If you don't have one, get one started. You can't do it alone. I was listening to a presentation by John C. Maxwell, and he said, "One is too small of a number to accomplish greatness." He gave further meaning to "TEAM" by using this pneumonic: "Together Everyone Achieves More." The African proverb says, "If you want to go fast, go alone; if you want to go far, go together."

THE WILL TO ACHIEVE GREAT THINGS

A great team made up of varying and different gifts will help you take your dream to the next level. Regardless of where you are, your journey to a fulfilled life or to greatness begins right where you are. All it takes for you to move forward is the WILL. Everything starts with it. Without it, nothing can happen! It doesn't matter how hard life has been to you, it takes a strong will and determination to improve your life. While life can be brutal, a lot of people would be more than willing to help you out if they see that you have the will, motivation, and right attitude to improve your life. There are great motivational books on the market that you can read to get you started.

This should be regarded as an investment in your development so that you can be guided to greatness and a fulfilled life. Any amount of money or time invested in yourself shouldn't be regarded as an expense. It's the greatest investment in you. You can also listen to podcasts based on your area of interest. Don't be afraid of technology. You can learn! In fact, since modern technology is here to stay, you may want to make up your mind to get by with it.

I've found that modern technology has made it much easier for us to acquire knowledge. Everything is at our fingertips. If you don't know about a particular subject that's of interest to you, research it by reading books or searching for great and reliable websites.

DEVELOP A NETWORK TO HELP YOU ACCOMPLISH YOUR DREAM

Don't underestimate the power of your network. You may already have a lot of well-meaning and inspiring people in your life. I've found that when I have a great idea, sharing it with the right people helps me to bring more clarity to it. They in turn help me to process some of the things I never thought of.

In my case, what I call my "dream lab" is my family: my wife, June, and our two daughters, Juneile and Nicole. This "dream lab" has helped me accomplish the dream that seemed rather impossible. As I share my dream with them, it helps me realize my areas of strengths and weaknesses. I can then tap into the right resources to help achieve my goals.

I like to listen to the people in my network of friends and acquaintances so that I can know more about them, like their strengths and areas of interest, and seek their help. It's very important to tap into the right resources. I don't like to talk to people about my dream lest they kill it before it's born. You must know your circle and who you can share your dreams with.

If my network doesn't have the expertise or the knowledge I need, I like to ask, "Who do you know who can assist?" You have to broaden your network as you go long. Don't wait until you need them to reach out to them. Contacting them when you don't necessarily need to tap into their resources will ensure that they don't feel like you're just using them to your advantage. Nurturing that friendship is key to a long-lasting relationship.

With your new sense of purpose, no one will come into your life without a reason, even if it's for a brief period. The key here is to grow your network. They may not be able to help you, but they may have someone in their network you need to know.

Make it your point of duty to save their contact details, either on your phone or in a notebook, with a description of their areas of expertise and interests. If you save their contact details on your phone, be sure you have a backup plan just in case you change or lose your phone.

To attract and keep the right people in your network, you must develop and maintain a winning attitude and a winsome personality. If you don't naturally possess these, don't worry. You can develop them by retraining the mind. Do a Google search or check Amazon to find books that can help you develop these great qualities. If you're going to attract the best, you must work on becoming your best. Great minds are attracted by great minds.

FOCUS ON YOUR DREAM

Regardless of how battered you are, you should not act like a victim. Just because you were victimized doesn't mean you must live like a victim. You must develop the mind of a victor.

Others will be attracted to you because when they listen to your story, it resonates with them. Better yet, it gives them hope. If life could have punched you in the gut, and you were knocked down yet found the strength and the courage to get up and continue the fight, those who have never been hit this hard will be attracted to you. And those who have been hit just as hard or harder will be even more attracted to you because you have something to offer them that they admire: "gumption." You may want to look up that word if it's new to you. To me, that's the inner fortitude that drives you—the will to thrive despite...

I've worked with individuals who have been used, abused, and overused. I can't recall anyone who had a rough life and a disturbing past playing the victim and succeeding. If you're going to be successful, you need to work on yourself to grow from where you are to where you need to be.

T.D. Jakes in his book, *Woman, Thou Art Loosed!* says, "To forgive is to break the link between you and your past. Sadly enough, many times the person hardest to forgive is the one in the mirror. Although they rage loudly about others, people secretly blame themselves for a failed relationship. Regardless of who you hold responsible, there is no healing in blame! When you begin to realize that your past does not necessarily dictate the outcome of your future, then you can release the hurt. It is impossible to inhale new air until you exhale the old... Exhale, then inhale; there is more for you."[1]

Life has been brutal, but you don't have to give up. To succeed, you must focus on your dream, surround yourself with the right people, read books that will inspire you, and take actions based on your dreams.

Many people inspire me to continue to fight the good fight of life. One of them is the inspiring story of someone I know, Dr. Bongelo Gombele. I would recommend his book to anyone who thinks that life is too hard and they cannot make it. He went through the worst of hardship and today, Bongelo Gombele is a medical doctor and surgeon. But if you were to read his book, *You Can Make It: The Inspiring Journey of One Man's Dream*, you'd be filled with courage and determination to not just survive but to thrive.

As a courageous adolescent, Dr. Bongelo Gombele decided to leave his hometown, Mbandaka, in the Democratic Republic of Congo, formerly known as Zaire, to begin a long yet perilous journey in more than twenty countries in four continents. He said "I overcame numerous obstacles, with determination to become a medical doctor."[2]

In his book, he shares how he succeeded in crossing the wilderness of the Sahara. How he was able to live in Sudan without speaking Arabic. How he landed in Jamaica without an address or a place to live. This is where I met him, as both of us were students at West Indies College, now Northern Caribbean University. At that time, we were both in our twenties. He had his own struggles, and I had mine. Among many things, we had two apparent things in common: One, we both were very poor with far more obstacles than we could count. Two, we both were determined not to allow our poverty and obstacles to steal away our determination to succeed. He was from the Democratic Republic of Congo, Africa, and I was from poverty-stricken Haiti. We knew what we wanted and what we needed to do. We went in search for that answer, and we got it. Today, we are both successful professionals. It all happened because of the WILL to be successful.

As a successful doctor and surgeon, Dr. Gombele will tell you that it all happened by the grace of God through the power of the will, and the determination to be successful. I too can tell you that after living in eleven countries in three continents, it was never easy, but looking back, I can say that it was worth fighting for. Today, I appreciate life. I have a better appreciation for those who are having a rough life yet are fighting tooth and nail to thrive. I'm grateful for the kind people God sent on my path who added value to my life.

I am determined to help anyone with a fighting spirit, because I was once where they are now. I was able to make it only because of the WILL to succeed and by the grace of God.

CHAPTER SUMMARY AND ACTION STEP

Reflect on this chapter. What does it mean to you? Remember, it's not what happened to you that matters the most but rather what happens within you.

Whether you or someone else is directly responsible for your misfortune don't lay blame. Take full responsibly to create your own world and future. Turn your bad circumstances in your favor, and your misfortune into a fortune. You will be stronger and better. Hopefully, you'll be more compassionate towards the less fortunate. Because you're standing on higher ground, you'll be able to pull up someone who's in their valley of despair, confusion, and misfortune. We are blessed to be a blessing to others. It's a privilege.

If you develop the will to thrive, you will make it, and you'll appreciate what you have even more. Never forget where you came from, and be prepared to mentor those who are struggling. Your blessings will multiply.

Are you going to put your dream to the acid test?

You were created to live a life full of dreams, but it's not enough to just dream; you need to take actions. What actions are you going to take to turn your dream into reality?

STEP 10:
REAPING THE BENEFITS
OF YOUR ACTION

Your success stories will be best appreciated when
painted with the brush of your own failures.
— Emile Maxi

DON'T BE AFRAID OF failures. Interview anyone who achieved anything worthwhile and they'll tell you that even the most calculated risks had to be dealt with in one way or another. You can't have success without failure. Regardless of what you do, there's a price to pay. If we dream big, we will reap its great and rewarding benefits. If we fail to dream big but live in the status quo, or the fear of failing, or playing it safe, it comes with a price tag also. In this case, you will never find your purpose in life. The ability to reach your full potential will disappear.

In his book *Chase the Lion*, Mark Batterson makes a provoking case for acting on our God-sized dreams. in the Lion Chaser's Manifesto, he writes:

"Quit living as if the purpose of life
is to arrive safely at death.
Run to the roar.
Set God-sized goals.
Pursue God given passions.
Go after a dream that is destined to
fail without divine intervention.
Stop pointing out problems,
become part of the solution.
Stop repeating the past, start creating the future.
Face your fears. Fight for your dreams.
Grab opportunities by the name and don't let go!
Live like today is the first and
last day of your life.
Burn sinful bridges. Blaze new trails.
Live for the applause of the nail-scarred hands.
Don't let what's wrong with you
keep you from worshiping what's right with God.
Dare to fail. Dare to be different.
Quit holding up. Quit holding
back. Quit running away.
Chase the Lion."[1]

As we conclude our journey through the pages of this book, I suggest that you "Chase the Lion," for whatever it's worth. What will prevent you from chasing your lion?

There are two kinds of people in this world:

- Those who make things happen
- Those who stand by and wonder why things are the way they are

Which of the two are you?

You started your life journey with dreams and a desire to accomplish great things. But along the way, you lost it. Something happened and took away the dream you once had. Are you satisfied to watch your once-cherished dream melt away? What are you going to do about it?

The first kind of people, those who make things happen, didn't achieve their dream because they're lucky. If you were to ask any successful person, or anyone who is climbing the ladder of success, they'd tell you that it's the result of hard work. Nothing in life comes easily. Anything worth fighting for will always be an uphill battle.

Why is there so much suffering in the world today? Why is there so much poverty? I often ask myself these questions. In fact, these questions seem to dominate the minds of people regardless of their race and social background.

Some people pray and wait for God to answer. They've waited for years for God to bless them financially, but to no avail. They've waited for years for God to bless their broken relationships, but to no avail. They end up casting blame and laying their lack of achievements on someone else. They fail to learn valuable lessons that even the birds can teach us. They are constantly in search for food, and they don't rest until it's time to. I have observed them very keenly. They are always on the move looking for food. I hardly see any of them sitting for any prolonged period without searching for food. To be searching for food is risky, as they make themselves a prey to other predators. But they do it anyway. What can we learn from them? Considering the lessons learned from these flying creatures, may I ask you a few questions?

- When we pray to God for financial blessings, does He shower down money on us? Or
- Does He give us the opportunities to work and the resources to be financially blessed?
- When we pray to God for courage, does He wave His magic wand and give us courage? Or
- Does He give us the opportunities to be courageous?
- When we pray to God for emotional and/or physical healing, does He stretch out His hand and heal us? Or
- Does He expect us to use the resources available to aid in our healing process?
- When we pray to God and ask Him to help us forgive the ones who harmed us, does He do it for us? Or
- Does He expect us to pass into action by granting forgiveness even when the person doesn't deserve it, so that we can experience inner peace?

You're already endowed with everything you need to succeed. The birds understand that God has already provided; it's their responsibility to exert the effort, go and look for food to nourish their bodies. What do they use to accomplish that? Their God-given abilities. They know that if they use their wings, they will take them where there is food. They know that if they use their little brain intelligence, it will guide them to the right place. But they also know that nothing in life comes without sacrifice. It's risky, but it must be done! To nurture themselves, they must act. To act is an action verb; nothing can be accomplished until they act. There's no need for them to worry, for God has already provided. Do they risk anything in the process of searching for food? Yes, their whole life!

WHAT DOES THIS MEAN FOR US?

By no means should we sit on the rocking chair swinging back and forth, hoping that it will take us somewhere, only to realize late in life that it's taking us nowhere. We should be actively involved in our own upliftment. We should address the things that need to be addressed to get us out of the rubble of life. We shouldn't pray and leave it to God to act for us. We shouldn't expect God to do what He has already done. He has given us all that we need to succeed. We must not wait. We must use our God-given abilities to help us to be what and who we were created to be.

If there is hunger and poverty in the world, it's not because of God but because we fail to act on what He has already blessed us with. Our ability to be and to do! It's all ours!

I'm aware that human greed and selfishness may make it more difficult to accomplish your dreams, but it's still possible. You just need to act.

So what's your dream? What's keeping you from reaching your God-given potential? Who is standing on your way? What is standing in your way? God has already granted you permission to remove the roadblocks. Move forward in His name! God is waiting for you to reap the harvest of your act of faith. He wants you to make your dream bigger than your size. He will fit you in over time!

God won't bless an investment you haven't started.

God won't make you reap a harvest you haven't planted.

God won't heal your emotional pain unless you let go of it.

God won't bless that business venture until you take that leap of faith.

God won't bless that relationship unless you put Him in it.

God won't forgive you unless you first forgive those who hurt you.

God won't set you free unless you first free yourself.

God won't open your "Red Sea" until you set both feet in the water.

God won't make your dream come to reality until you act on it.

Let nothing stop you.

Go, act on it now!

CONCLUSION

THE ISSUES OF THE heart and the issues of the mind are interwoven. You cannot separate them. The issues of the mind are the product of the issues of the heart. Failing to address the issues of the heart will result in constant pain and suffering. Therefore, the mind will suffer, which will result in the inability to be all that we were created to be.

Why is there so much hurt in the world today? It's because of the unresolved issues of the heart. The overwhelming feeling will express itself in your speech and in your action. The tongue becomes the most lethal weapon, with the power to mess up lives for a lifetime. Until we learn to deal with and resolve our emotional pain, our mind will always be derailed. Hence, we will always be contributing to the pain of the ones we love, and the pain of society.

You've been hurt many times over. Your heart is broken and scarred. Your mind is in a state of total confusion and bewilderment. What will you do about it? The solution to the issues of your heart and mind lies in your power.

My hope and prayer are that you will take the steps necessary to heal your heart from any unresolved grief and emotional pain so that your mind can do what it was created to do—dream and accomplish God-sized dreams. Your heart and your mind work like hands and gloves. Both need to be in perfect synchronization to function properly.

What issues do you need to address? Dealing with them should be your top priority. This will free your mind to take you to where you've always wanted to be but lacked the courage and mental fortitude to go there.

I hope this process was helpful to you. If for any reason you find that you are still suffering from the emotional pain, and you aren't able move forward, don't despair. You went through a lot of emotional pain over the years. It will take time to get over it. Continue to put into practice the advice of this book, and keep evaluating yourself for progress. Keep working on yourself and your own healing process. You deserve to be emotionally free and to do the things you've always dreamed of.

May God bless you and heal you and grant you God-sized dreams!

ABOUT THE AUTHOR

EMILE MAXI IS A pastor, marriage officer and counselor, life coach, and Grief Recovery specialist. He has served as a pastor for over thirty years, working in the Caribbean, Central America, the South Pacific, and North America. He holds a Bachelor's degree in Theology and a Master's degree in Education.

Pastor Maxi takes pleasure in helping people deal with their emotional issues so that they can free themselves to be the best that God created them to be as they discover their dreams and live lives of meaning and purpose.

The services offered by the author include:

- Grief Recovery Sessions—This is a seven-week, one hour per week program that focuses on addressing the unresolved issues of the heart, which may be due to separation, divorce, the death of a loved-one, the loss of health, the loss of financial resources, moving, and emotional issues, just to name a few.

- Life Coaching—This is a ten-week, one hour per week program that focuses on helping individuals move forward in life based on their dreams and aspirations.
- Marital Counselling Sessions—This is a seven-week program that focuses on pre-marital counselling or post-marital counselling sessions to help couples navigate through their marital issues.

If I can be of further assistance to you, please do not hesitate to email me at: emaxibooks@gmail.com

Or visit our website at: emaxibooks.com

NOTES

Chapter 1

1. M. Scott Peck, *The Road Less Traveled* (New York: Touchstone, 2003), 15.
2. www.merriam-webster.com/dictionary/health
3. John W. James and Russel Friedman, *The Grief Recovery Handbook* (New York: Harper-Collins, 2009), 9.
4. Nelson Mandela, *Long Walk to Freedom* (New York: Back Bay Books, 1995).
5. Grace A. Kelly, *Grieve if You Must* (Jamaica: Northern Caribbean University Press, 2011), 96
6. John W. James and Russel Friedman, *The Grief Recovery Handbook* (New York: Harper-Collins, 2009), 9.

Chapter 2

1. www.goodreads.com/quotes/tag/present
2. Ibid
3. Ibid
4. Ibid

5. Eckhart Tolle, *The Power of Now: A Guide to Spiritual Enlightenment* (Namaste Publishing, 2004), 35–36.

6. John W. James and Russel Friedman, *The Grief Recovery Handbook* (New York: Harper-Collins, 2009), 78.

7. Ibid., 3.

Chapter 3

1. John C. Maxwell, *Developing the Leader Within You 2.0* (Harper Collins Leadership, 2018), 1

2. Isaiah 1:17 ESV

Chapter 4

1. 1 Samuel 17:33 NLT

2. 1 Samuel 17:54b NLT

3. Franklin D. Roosevelt, Inaugural Address, March 4, 1933, as published in Samuel Rosenman, ed., *The Public Papers of Franklin D. Roosevelt, Volume Two: The Year of Crisis, 1933* (New York: Random House, 1938), 11–16.

Chapter 5

1. 1 John 1:9 NIV

2. Matthew 7:12 NIV

3. 1 Peter 3:9 NIV

4. Matthew 7:13 NIV

Chapter 6

1. www.history.com/news/10-things-you-may-not-know-about-the-wright-brothers

Chapter 8

1. montyroberts.com
2. www.jfklibrary.org/node/16986
3. www.npr.org/2010/01/18/122701268/i-have-a-dream-speech-in-its-entirety

Chapter 9

1. T.D. Jakes, *Woman, Thou Art Loosed!* (Destiny Image Publishers, Inc.: PA, 2012), 19.
2. Bongelo Gombele, *You Can Make It: The Inspiring Journey of One Man's Dream* (Jamaica, 2006), 1.

Chapter 10

1. Mark Batterson, *Chase the Lion: If Your Dream Doesn't Scare you, it's Too Small* (Crown Publishing Group, a division of Penguin Random House: NY, 2016), viiii